Celebrating Planet Earth, a Pagan/Christian Conversation:

First Steps in Inter-faith Dialogue

Celebrating Planet Earth, a Pagan/Christian Conversation:

First Steps in Inter-faith Dialogue

Edited by Denise Cush

Winchester, UK
Washington, USA

First published by Moon Books, 2015
Moon Books is an imprint of John Hunt Publishing Ltd., Laurel House, Station Approach,
Alresford, Hants, SO24 9JH, UK
office1@jhpbooks.net
www.johnhuntpublishing.com
www.moon-books.net

For distributor details and how to order please visit the 'Ordering' section on our website.

Text copyright: Denise Cush 2014

ISBN: 978 1 78279 830 9
Library of Congress Control Number: 2014958371

A CIP catalogue record for this book is available from the British Library.

Design: Stuart Davies
www.stuartdaviesart.com

Printed and bound by CPI Group (UK) Ltd, Croydon, CR0 4YY, UK

We operate a distinctive and ethical publishing philosophy in all
areas of our business, from our global network of authors to
production and worldwide distribution.

CONTENTS

Information about contributors

Philip Carr-Gomm is leader of the worldwide Order of Bards, Ovates and Druids, the largest Druid organisation. He is well known for his writing on Druidry and related spirituality.

Alison Eve Cudby is a co-founder of Forest Church, ritualist for Ancient Arden Forest Church, and a professional musician, singer and songwriter. She also follows the Ceilé Dé tradition.

Denise Cush is Professor of Religion and Education at Bath Spa University, and has published research on young Pagans and on Christians in Britain, as well as Buddhism, Hinduism and Religious Education.

Graham Harvey is Reader in Religious Studies at the Open University and author of many books on Paganism, indigenous religions and the academic study of religion.

Steve Hollinghurst is a freelance researcher, consultant and trainer in contemporary culture, evangelism and new forms of church within that context. He has had a particular focus on researching new spiritualities and contemporary Paganism for the past 20 years.

Simon Howell was, at the time of the Conversation, Team Vicar in the parish of Keynsham and Inter-faith Adviser in the Diocese of Bath and Wells. He is now Team Vicar and Pioneer Minister in Stroud, Gloucestershire.

Viannah Rain is the Pagan Federation's Inter-faith Officer in Devon and Cornwall.

Philip Shallcrass (Greywolf) is a writer, musician, singer-songwriter, artist and chief of the British Druid Order (BDO). He writes a blog, Greywolf's Lair, which can be found at: http://greywolf.druidry.co.uk/

Bruce Stanley is the pioneer of Forest Church and author of *Forest Church: A Field Guide to Nature Connection for Groups and Individuals.*

Tess Ward is a hospice chaplain, retreat leader and author of *The Celtic Wheel of the Year: Celtic and Christian Seasonal Prayers.*

Liz Williams is a Druid and professional writer who writes for the Guardian and runs a shop in Glastonbury.

Acknowledgement

The authors would like to thank Benedicte Scholefield and all the staff at the Ammerdown Centre for providing us with the ideal setting in which to conduct the Conversation.

Chapter 1

Introduction: Setting the scene, issues and challenges, overview and editorial reflections

Denise Cush

The idea for this book came from a weekend spent at the Ammerdown Centre (31st January – 2nd February 2014), when a group of nearly forty Pagans and Christians were invited to take part in a 'Conversation' in a place dedicated to dialogue, reconciliation and renewal. Initially seen as a Druid/Christian dialogue, the Pagan contribution widened to include Wiccans and other Pagans. The hope was that the participants could explore their prejudices and preconceptions, learn more about each other, and find common ground in 'Celebrating Planet Earth', as the event was called. Although this was not the first time that Christians and Pagans have attempted dialogue, all involved felt that something new and special had occurred, which could be built upon. The contributors to the book either gave talks during the Conversation or were present as participants with particular expertise. The proposed book seeks to capture the insights of the weekend and point to some ways forward.

We hope that the book will be of interest to Pagans and Christians interested in making connections, to academics and undergraduate students in Study of Religions taking courses on inter-faith dialogue, Paganism and Christianity and anyone with an interest in inter-faith activities. Some of the contributors are academics in the field, but as well as academic input, there is a practical emphasis on personal spirituality and ritual practice.

I was invited to be the 'impartial chair' of the Conversation,

1

and subsequently editor of the book, as someone with academic (and some experiential) knowledge of both traditions, but currently identifying as neither Pagan nor Christian. My research has included fieldwork with Christians from diverse denominations, and young people who identified as Witches and Pagans. My own religious background was Roman Catholic, but I would describe myself as a 'pluralist agnostic', finding wisdom in a variety of religious and non-religious worldviews.

My initial reaction to the idea of the Conversation was that there would be a number of issues and challenges to face in attempting to bring Christians and Pagans together over a shared concern for the natural environment. It is important to clarify our terminology, and ensure that our use of terms such as 'Pagan', 'Druid', 'Witch', 'Christian' are carefully defined when they can carry very different meanings. Such terms often come with 'baggage' and elicit stereotypes. The history of encounters between Pagans and Christians over the past 2,000 years has tended to the negative, from the early Christian martyrs to the accusations of 'Satanic' ritual abuse of children in the 1980s and 90s. This unfortunate 'real' history has been exacerbated by the 'imagined' history such as Margaret Murray's (1921) theory that many of those burned as witches by Christian authorities in late medieval and early modern times were actually Pagans who had kept going an underground, unbroken tradition since the conversion of European countries to Christianity. It is a human tendency to define oneself over against 'the other', and Christians and Pagans have been the 'other' against which identities have been constructed. Early Christians had to distinguish themselves from both Jews and pagans, and in doing so created negative pictures of these 'others'. This could even be said to start when Jesus himself, when advising his followers about prayer, said (according to Matthew's gospel) 'do not babble as the pagans do' (Matthew 6.7). In a similar way, some contemporary Pagans tend to define themselves in contrast with the predominantly Christian culture, seen as patriarchal and planet-destroying.

Section A: Addressing our fears and prejudices

The first section of the book explores further the fears, prejudices and imagined histories that each side has held against the other, as it was felt important to acknowledge and explore these issues first, in order to distinguish stereotypes and misunderstandings from real points of debate between the traditions. It recognises that even using terms like 'Christian' and 'Pagan' suggests that these are neat, definable categories and fails to emphasise that neither so-called tradition is monolithic and indeed each is in itself very diverse. Some Pagans and some Christians may have more in common with each other than their co-religionists.

Steve Hollinghurst writes from a Christian perspective. He examines the 'mythic histories' that each side tells about the other and explores how far these stereotyped pictures measure up to what can be known from historical research. History reveals a more complex picture of relationships and mutual influences between various Christian and Pagan groups in different times and places. There have indeed been what might be euphemistically called unfortunate encounters, but myths such as that of the 'burning times' need to be cleared out of the way if there is to be any mutual understanding. An important part of dealing with fears and prejudices is realising that both 'Paganism' and 'Christianity' are very diverse, both over time and in the present, so that any statement about either tradition needs at least to be qualified by the word 'some'. Steve goes on to look at Christian attitudes towards 'other' religions more generally, and demonstrates that they are very varied. He employs the now familiar terminology of 'exclusivist', 'inclusivist' and 'pluralist' (a typology that originated with Alan Race, 1983) to categorise attitudes, divides 'pluralist' into 'modern' and 'postmodern' varieties, and adds his own 'transformational' approach. This reminded me of my own 1994 typology (Cush, 1994), in which I also subdivided the traditional three categories, and suggested my own 'positive pluralist' approach, which is not too dissimilar from the 'transformational' approach, but without a Christian theological underpinning. We share the idea that only someone already at the top of the mountain is in a position to claim that all paths eventually get there – meanwhile we less elevated mortals may be able to learn much from those on other paths.

Graham Harvey, writing from an animist Pagan perspective, examines some of the clichéd preconceptions that each side has had of the other. Humour can play an important role in taking the sting out of stereotypes. He also warns us not to rush into false claims of unity, which tend to presume others are more like us 'really' than they actually are. It is important (and more interesting) to acknowledge and discuss real disagreements. Whilst acknowledging the diversity in each tradition, he uses the motifs of 'salvation' and 'enchantment' to explore some of the real differences between the two traditions. The separation of 'nature' and 'culture' is challenged, and the importance of seeing humans as part of a web of human and other-than-human relationships is stressed. Both Christians and Pagans share a common home and ecology, threatened by capitalist modernity and its managerial bureaucracy. Ritual can play an important part in strengthening our relationships with our other-than-human neighbours, and both Pagans and Christians need to be in the world as full participants, working, as well as just talking, together.

Section B: Possibilities for co-operation

Having, we hoped, cleared away some of the misconceptions that can get in the way of dialogue, and laughing together about some of the more ridiculous of these, the Conversation moved on to examining what the prospects might be for co-operation. In the second section, two Christians and two Druids suggest some positive ways forward.

Liz Williams examines some of the reasons why Paganism is growing in popularity – these include the lack of dogmatism, and tolerance of diversity. Significantly, 'its eclecticism, and often its refusal to take itself too seriously, are appealing to a generation raised on media fantasy which rejects hierarchical and dogmatic movements.' Rejecting the claims of an unbroken ancient tradition, and indeed, pointing to some Christian influences on magical and Pagan practices, she traces the roots of much in contemporary Wicca and Druidry to concepts and figures in the imagination of 19th century poets and novelists. A recurrent theme in this book is the importance and power of story, whether ancient myth or modern romance, in providing the materials to fashion contemporary beliefs and practices. In drawing upon literary sources, it seems to the current editor that contemporary Paganism in its adult form does after all have something in common with the 'Pop Culture Paganism' growing among younger adherents, who add to ancient myth and modern novels, figures and ideas drawn from film, television, graphic novels and digital resources (for information on Pop Culture Paganism see for example the blog at thepaganstudygroup, 2014; I would also like to record a thanks to my student Bryony Vine for alerting me to this particular self-designation to describe the phenomenon). From a Pagan and Druid perspective, Liz can identify several areas where Christians and Pagans share common ground. These include sacred places, seasonal festivals, social action to aid others, care for the environment and the very recognition that there is a divine or a spiritual dimension. Where there is goodwill, there are several possibilities for co-operation.

Myths in the sense of false information, especially ones with negative consequences, need to be exposed and rejected. However, another sense of the term 'myth' is that of a significant story, through which we explore our deepest feelings about the most important aspects of life. The 'literal' truth of such stories is irrelevant, one way or the other, what matters is the meaning conveyed (see for example Armstrong, 2000, on 'mythos' and 'logos' in the ancient world). **Simon Howell** employs this positive understanding of myth in exploring the value of – possibly 'mythical' – Golden Ages in inter-faith relationships. Even if historical research casts doubt upon an idyllic 11th century Toledo or an Iron Age Celtic Britain where Pagans and Christians lived in harmony with nature and each other, the inspiring myths of writers such as John Michell can provide us with a vision of what might be, in this case Pagans and Christians sharing a concern and working in mutual co-operation for the planet that all inhabit. Our ancient 'Celtic Connections' may be in part fantasy, but can still provide a powerful mythology to influence the future. Both traditions have a notion of the veil between this world and the otherworld of deeper reality, and consider that at certain times this veil can be very thin. Sharing our stories, poetry, songs and rituals can bring about moments of transcendence where what might have been or might one day be, becomes, if only for a moment, a present reality.

Philip Carr-Gomm takes the ideas of shared roots and inspiring myth and stories a stage further to examine whether as well as co-operation and mutual learning between Pagans and Christians there might even be new spiritual paths that fuse elements of each. Realising that some Druids and Christians would find this unacceptable, he explores examples where individuals and groups have made coherent spiritualities that draw upon both traditions. He points out that combining Pagan and Christian ideas and practices is not a new idea. In fact the origins of contemporary Druidry in the 17th and 18th centuries were in Christian circles, and there were many Christian influences on Wicca. As neo-Paganism struggled to define itself in the last few decades of the 20th century, it consciously differentiated itself from Christianity, but now should be confident enough of itself to draw nearer. One real difference is found in the historical claims of orthodox Christianity, whereas Paganism is more comfortable with accepting their stories as 'myth' (in the positive sense). Philip sees the Forest Church movement as an exciting new development drawing upon both traditions. Although this movement (see chapter 9) does not set out to be a syncretism of Christianity and Paganism, but rather emphasises the need to participate in, and seek the divine in, nature, it is open to other earth-based spiritualities, and some rituals used draw directly upon Druid and Wiccan models. Another example that explicitly draws upon both Christianity and Druidry is the Celtic Orthodox Church in Brittany. The current editor tends to avoid the word 'syncretism' as it might suggest the combination of two fixed and bounded traditions. However, it will be interesting to see what new and creative combinations of already diverse and fluid Christian and Pagan traditions, and indeed hybrids and fusions will emerge and, whether welcomed or not, this is happening already.

In fact, the chapter that follows is an example of one person's experience of the transformative power of a spirituality able to draw upon both Pagan and Christian sources.

Tess Ward shares with us how the discovery of earth-centred Pagan traditions enabled her to come through a difficult period in her life into a renewed, deeper and more compassionate Christian faith. This journey may need to be replicated by the Christian tradition more widely, which may even have to die in its old, patriarchal, nature-neglecting form in order to be resurrected into a new, earth-centred faith. We considered it important to include personal experience in this book for several reasons. Religion is so often better expressed in poetry, story, silence, ritual and action than in academic philosophy and theology. In most forms of contemporary Paganism, human experience is a main source of authority, as well as listening to the other-than-human world. Similarly, feminists both Christian and Pagan have emphasised the authority of women's experience (for example, Isherwood and McEwan, 1993, pp.79-80, Reid-Bowen, 2007, pp.44-45), a crucial source of authority as women have tended not to be the major spokespersons or authors of sacred texts in more established religions.

Section C: The role of ritual practice, story, music and poetry in inter-faith encounter

Not only did the speakers emphasise the importance of story, poetry, ritual, being outside in nature, and silence in their own traditions, and in inter-faith encounters, but during the weekend Conversation, we (whether Pagan, Christian or neither) had several occasions to participate in shared ritual and/or meditation and music. Hence it was felt important to include reflections on the role of ritual, story, poetry and music in such encounters in this book. Shared ritual is often more controversial in inter-faith work than meeting for discussion in order to under-stand each others' beliefs and worldviews better, and may not always be thought appropriate. However, on the other hand, in the history of most religions, ritual, story and song were prior to the working out of systematic theologies and so sharing these can be seen as a more appropriate first step in inter-faith encounter than theological debates, and more likely to enable an empathetic understanding.

Viannah Rain shares with us four examples of rituals that illustrate the use of myth, symbol and nature in a way that is in large part common to Druids, Wiccans and some other Pagans. These are the Circle, the importance of participation, dressing up as deities and 'sharing cakes and ale'. She stresses the 'performative' nature of ritual, which brings about transformation, and the importance of relationships with others and with nature. Pagan festivals follow the rhythms of the natural world, as in the well-known 'wheel of the year', the eight seasonal festivals, many of which coincide with Christian festivals. Again the poetic truth embodied in myth is an important motif, as is the psychological

8

power of symbolic ritual, and the inspiration that both can bring. The examples given all stress the importance of embodied existence and connection with nature. As Christians and Pagans share much cultural history it may be possible to design rituals meaningful to both. Viannah considers that perhaps Paganism has something to offer Christianity in allowing it to discover (or perhaps re-discover) the sacredness of nature and power of ritual.

The Reformation and the Enlightenment in Western Europe gradually, in the term popularised by Max Weber, 'disenchanted' the universe. As a result, the power of ritual, as well as the connection between human and non-human nature, has perhaps been neglected by the more protestant wing of Christianity. Paganism can offer a 're-enchantment' that gives meaning to life via ritual. A feature that strikes the outsider is that Pagan ritual has much scope for individual and group creativity in that participants are free to create their own new rituals.

Bruce Stanley, pioneer of the 'Forest Church' movement, also creates new rituals and experiential exercises, with the purpose of enabling people not just to be in nature, but also to participate in nature. Although Forest Church practices sometimes resemble or draw upon Pagan patterns, for Bruce the important thing is connection with and participation in nature, and through this participation to both connect with God and gain a deep motivation to care for the planet. There are some Druid influences, but Forest Church is not an attempt to create a syncretistic movement. Though open to all, his Forest Church is clearly rooted in what he calls 'the Christ Tradition', an expression he prefers to 'Christianity' because of the 'baggage' associated with the latter term. Some of the exercises in the Forest Church book resemble bushcraft on the one hand or 'experiential' religious education lessons on the other, but all seek to reconnect people whether Christian, Pagan or of no religion with nature – not a place or a thing, but a 'process of complex inter-relationships'.

Bruce and Viannah describe innovative practices from within the Pagan and Christian traditions, and invite the 'other' tradition to join in. However, there have been attempts to deliberately create inter-faith rituals that draw Christians and Pagans together. **Greywolf (Philip Shallcrass)** describes one such initiative taken over 20 years ago, the Avebury Gorsedd in 1993. This brought together various Pagan groups with Christians and others in a ceremony that all found valuable. Greywolf provides us with some of the text of the ritual, which was carefully worded so that different traditions could understand it in their own way. It is fascinating to learn that part of the script written for this ceremony was used in the closing ceremony for the Paralympics in 2012, a perfect illustration of a prayer originating in Druidry having something to offer those of all religions and none. As in Viannah's examples, the circle, the four directions, myth, symbol, poetry, creativity and inspiration (the *awen* of the Druidic bard) are vitally important in the ceremony. It is the power of poetry, music and creative arts more generally that speaks across traditions, allowing all to join in in a way that would be impossible with, for example, reciting a creed viewed as doctrinal propositions. Greywolf also speaks movingly of the Christian/Druid funeral arranged for his wife, the two examples showing that shared ritual can actually work.

Alison Eve Cudby and Paul Cudby arranged the ceremonies and music over the weekend, designed to be shared by both Christians and Pagans. Alison reflects on this experience and discusses how far shared ritual can actually work. Questions arise such as whether Christian use of Pagan elements is appropriate or appropriation. Some of the meaning of a ritual may be shared, but other aspects may be given different meanings by different participants. Some within both traditions may be very critical of attempts to share ritual, especially if ritual is seen as the unambiguous expression of doctrines. However, if ritual is seen as performative and transformative then perhaps theological differences can be put to one side and the power of symbol, myth, music and action can create a valuable experience for a diverse group, and one that actually achieves something, especially in the area of celebrating planet earth and reconnecting with nature.

The idea that ritual 'works' in this sense of actually achieving something is one shared by Catholic Christians, Pagans, practitioners of magic and many religious traditions. Whether the transformation is in the mind of the participant or in the external world is debated, but perhaps this distinction breaks down anyway.

Most of the material in Section C reflects what Christians can learn from Pagan use of ritual. Could the process also work the other way round? Shared ritual goes a stage further in inter-faith encounter than simply learning about each others' traditions and using such knowledge to get beyond prejudices. However, along with shared practical, ethical and social action, it is probably more accessible than the attempt to construct shared theology, a project beyond the scope of a single weekend.

Section

A

Addressing our fears and prejudices

Chapter 2

No-one expects the Spanish Inquisition! Understanding how Pagans and Christians can see each other today through the distorted lenses of their mythic histories

Steve Hollinghurst

The shadow of the Burning Times

On several occasions Pagans I have met, on discovering I am Christian, have said, 'You people burnt our ancestors'. I usually apologise for what some Christians did in the past to people they called witches and suggest that Christians and Pagans today need to learn to understand each other so that we can overcome the prejudices that led to such events.

It is still true today that anyone calling themselves Pagan, especially anyone claiming to be a witch, may well meet prejudice. My response is based on the assumption that any Pagan who raises witch-burning fears that prejudice is what they will receive from me as a Christian and I want to allay that fear. But I could treat the statement as a historical claim and suggest that the story of the 'burning times' is not what is often assumed. At various times and places in the past people have been burnt for being witches; however, most of this was not carried out by the church. Indeed, much of it was carried out either before Christianity or in non-Christian countries. Further, that a modern Pagan is really an inheritor of the traditions of a mediaeval witch is also highly debateable. We are dealing here with a mythic history in which the Spanish Inquisition in some versions burnt as many witches as the number of Jews who died in the Second World War.

Sadly, in reality, the Spanish Inquisition was not like the

Monty Python sketch in which they torture an elderly lady suspected of being a witch by putting her in the comfy chair and poking her with cushions. The reality is also far from the myth. Indeed, as is argued by historians like Ronald Hutton (1991), persecution of witches was common in pre-Christian Europe until it was outlawed by Christians, who in the earlier years of the faith taught that witchcraft was not real. Later, this position changed, and from about the 13th century onwards there were Christians teaching that witches could receive power from the devil. This opened the way for a renewal of witchcraft persecution. Even then this was at its most virulent in areas where the church had little control. During the centuries of witch trials in Europe somewhere between 40,000 and 60,000 people were executed. Most of the deaths were as a result of cases brought by ordinary people in secular local courts (see for instance Behringer, 2004, and Scarre and Callow, 2001). Within this total the Spanish Inquisition executed at most 5,000, 2%-3% of those accused, most of whom were Jews forcibly converted to Christianity who carried on Jewish practice (See for instance Kamen, 1997 and Rawlings, 2006). This is, of course, still a bad legacy and one for which a change in Christian teaching bears some responsibility. On these grounds I am happy to offer my condemnation of past Christian action to today's Pagans. But the truth is not as the myth would have it.

Anthropologists like Mary Douglas (1973) would argue that witch hunting seems to be a sociological issue. In Douglas's schema societies are structured along two axes, 'Group' and 'Grid'. The former indicates emphasis on the collective, strong 'Group', or individual, weak 'Group'. The latter indicates the emphasis on hierarchy and power, strong 'Grid', or the lack of these, weak 'Grid'. In societies that have an important 'Group' element yet a lack of strong hierarchical 'Grid', witchcraft is often used to explain the threat of others to the group's identity, which is not rigidly defined by social structure. The traits of a 'witch-hunting' society are for Douglas: a distrust of civil power; an emphasis on charismatic leadership and a mistrust of internal hierarchy; an emphasis on the spiritual and denigration of the physical; a view of those inside the group as pure and holy whilst those outside are witches dwelling in an evil and hostile world; a stress on rigidly orthodox behaviour and belief. Often of course, religious belief can be used to bolster such social tensions, but the beliefs themselves do not explain such tensions.

As mentioned above, witch hunting precedes Christianity. Pre-Christian Rome expressed it within the crime of *Lucerna Extincta*, 'lights out', a clandestine ceremony in which the participants allegedly went to an underground place, often a cave, extinguished the lights, had a sexual orgy, and then met nine months later to sacrifice the babies so produced (see Eliade 1976, pp.69-92). One group of people often accused of this crime were Christians, who did meet in catacombs and allegedly drank human blood. However much a Christian communion celebration might be misinterpreted this way, it is a classic way to label them as outcasts to be feared or loathed (Eliade 1976, pp.69-92). At the height of the early modern witch craze, descriptions of the supposed witches' sabbat are a version of this crime. Indeed such accusations surfaced again during the investigations of alleged satanic ritual abuse during the late 1980s. In places suspicions during this fell on contemporary Pagans, raising fears that the 'burning times' might return in a modern form.

If the stereotyping of witches has passed from pagan to Christian and led to persecutions on both sides it is also true that issues of power have contributed to this. So the gradual acceptance of Christianity as state religion by successive Roman Emperors also led to Christian suppression of other faiths. With some periods of repression, Jews had received tolerance from the Emperors prior to Christian acceptance. The church increasingly opposed such tolerance. During the reign of Theodosius, 379-395, for instance a North African Christian mob incited by the local bishop looted and destroyed a Jewish Synagogue at Callinicum (see Chadwick 1967, pp.167-170 and Lee 2013). The Emperor felt this was criminal activity and ordered the church to pay reparations to the Jewish community. Bishop Ambrose of Milan insisted the church would do no such thing and threatened to excommunicate the Emperor if he pressed his case. The Emperor backed down. Later as Christianity was established as the religion of all Romans by the edict of Justinian in 529, Jews alone were officially exempt from becoming Christians (Code of Justinian 1.11.10). However, it was not unknown for Jews to be forcibly baptized anyway; a practice that would become more prevalent over time. Christianity, a once persecuted Jewish sect, had by this time become a Greco-Roman faith that persecuted Jews. From the establishment of the Holy Roman Empire in 800 under Charlemagne it also increasingly coupled religious conversion with invasion and forced baptism. This is hardly a history of tolerance even when the church was teaching against witchcraft persecution.

When speaking at events on contemporary Paganism I have often been asked by Christians about an allegation that witches are meeting to cast curses on the Christian family, putting these on cassette tape in trees outside churches or Christian homes, or on roadsides to cause accidents (just Google this to find articles about it). I can't find any reason to see this as anything but a sinister reading of a natural phenomenon, and note that with the demise of the cassette, plastic bags have taken their place. Firstly if anyone did want to curse someone, and I know people who do believe cursing is sometimes justified, this seems an odd and very random way to do it. More worryingly, the assumption that there are people causing harm by witchcraft is the kind of thinking that lay behind the very witch hunts we have just discussed.

As Pagans and Christians seek to understand each other better there are fears and prejudices both sides bring with them.

Some of these may be based on real issues, but most are the result of our respective mythic histories. Both communities need to recognise these for what they are and seek out the genuine issues our communities need to explore. However, these mythic histories run deep and need handling respectfully. Underneath them may be real events turned into the mythic version of today. Also these stories are felt strongly because they are linked to real fears and hopes, and these too must be taken seriously. So let us trace some of our respective mythic histories and hope that behind them we can get to the real issues that matter.

Christian and Pagan mythic histories

The outlines I give are caricatures; they may raise a smile, but will be recognisable to both communities. Both have some truth in them, but have become part of a mythic history. As such they are part of each community's identity and one that sees both communities as historical enemies when the reality is often more complex.

The Christian narrative begins with Jewish mythic history. Jewish religious identity was formed against a backdrop of Ancient Near-Eastern paganism, especially Canaanite (I am here following the convention that contemporary Pagans and Paganism have a capital letter as they are the name of a religion, ancient paganism has no capital as it is a label given by later writers). This history depicts the people within the land that would become Israel as polytheistic pagans seeking to appease their gods by offering child sacrifices and indulging in ritual sex. For this corruption the Jewish scriptures claim God gives power to the Jews so they can conquer them and take their land. In this mythic history within this corrupt pagan world the one true God exposes the false gods of paganism and gives the law through Moses so that the Jews become a beacon of good in a corrupt world. However, they themselves are constantly fighting the corrupting influence of surrounding pagan nations, a temptation they sometimes give into with severe consequences. Ultimately God's plan to bring light to the world unfolds in Jesus and his followers who take the good news to the surrounding pagan countries. Indeed, as they do so we again find Christians driving out pagan customs and setting people free from superstition, idolatry and evil demonic forces. But if the nations gradually become Christian there remain occultists and witches who follow the devil and perform evil magic, seeking to thwart the Christians, though they can never win as God's victory is assured.

The contemporary Pagan version tells its mythic history from a rather different perspective. In this mythic history there was a time when all the world was pagan and people lived in harmony with the land and respected nature and all life. Women were equal with men in all things including divinity. But then came the angry Sky God of the Jews and their monotheistic beliefs and attacked the noble pagan way of life. This new faith taught that there was only one true belief and that the earth was given to humans as something to use for their benefit. This faith was then taken up by Christians who took it round the world driving out local belief and culture and taking ancient pagan sacred sites and festivals into Christianity. It became an imperial religion and Christian armies went out attacking other faith groups and conquering and forcibly converting pagans. They introduced patriarchy and abused nature and made religion all about getting to heaven after you die. But in secret people kept the old pagan faith and passed it on to new generations. These people have been persecuted by Christians, especially during the 'burning times'. However, from this a new Paganism has begun to flourish, offering hope of a return to tolerance and living well as part of nature.

Both mythic histories are a mix of real events and simplification, embellishment and interpretation. As we have already seen from a brief exploration of early modern witch hunts the reality is often complex. Often there is a limited amount of evidence. Until recently we relied heavily on Jewish Scripture for an understanding of ancient Canaanite religion. These talk of the sacrifice of children to Molech, ritual prostitution and the frenzied rites of those in the religion. Examples of this can be found in Leviticus 18.3, 22-25, Deuteronomy 9.4-5 and 1 Kings 18.28. What can be noted from such passages is also that they functioned both as a justification for the formation of the nation of Israel and for Jewish separation from the surrounding nations. They thus form a powerful part of Jewish national and religious identity. The very negative view of the Biblical account was also backed up by later Greek and Roman sources like Herodotus who wrote about ritual prostitution in the region (*Histories* 1.199).

More recent archaeology and especially the discovery of more durable cuneiform tablets of writing at Ras Shamra have enabled a rediscovery of Canaanite descriptions of their religion. There is considerable debate around how this should be viewed. There is a recognition, at the very least, that the biblical account, and that of Herodotus, is greatly exaggerated. Some scholars have become convinced that neither human sacrifice nor sacred prostitution or ritual marriage were part of Canaanite religion at all. Others think these were occasional ritual acts and may have been symbolic rather than actual. Interestingly, some contemporary Pagans have created *Natib Qadish*, a modern Pagan faith drawing on the Ras Shamra texts (see Budin 2008, Wyatt 2003, Day 2004).

Biblical scholarship has become increasingly aware of the way Judaism itself emerges from a polytheistic Canaanite religious background. The pre-mosaic Patriarchs do not after the call of Abraham abandon all their old religious beliefs and customs. Indeed it is Abraham who thinks he has been called to sacrifice his son Isaac and discovers that Yahweh doesn't want this (Genesis 22.1-19). This story makes sense if there was some belief in child sacrifice as a practice. Similarly it is several generations before Abraham's descendants get rid of their household gods

(Genesis 35.2). From this gradual movement towards monotheism the creation story emerges as an adaptation of that in which Baal makes the world. The name of the chief of the Canaanite pantheon, El, becomes the word for God in Hebrew scripture. It is interesting to note in the light of this that later Jewish commentators on Genesis (Rabbah 38) add a story about Abraham destroying the idol workshop of his father Terah. Adding Midrash in this way often in the margins of the text is a common part of Jewish practice, but this story may be seen as countering the impression given by the text of a slow move away from polytheism (see Moberly 2001, McCurley 1983, Hollinghurst 2010, pp.101-105).

The situation is more complex when looking at northern European paganism. Again there is a shortage of records from people like British Druids, leaving us to rely on accounts from Caesar's *The Gallic Wars* book VI or the works of Tacitus. These are rather like the early Jewish texts in that they justify the idea of the 'improvement' of the Gauls' and Britons' lives under Roman occupation. We are also reliant on the lives of the Christian missionaries who converted them. Some of these, like the Jewish accounts, suggest changing views of paganism over time. Later 7th century lives of St Patrick by Tírechán and Muirchu both portray the saint in almost military terms fighting the Druids, in contrast to the more gentle tone of Patrick's own surviving letters and the few earlier pieces which suggest a far more positive attitude (see De Paor 1993, Hutton 2007, pp.93-136). In researching the lives of some of the earliest Celtic saints one is struck by how often they encounter dragons. Such tales are quite likely to reflect Christian encounters with pagan sacred sites and indeed their pagan guardians. If later accounts have Christian saints slaying dragons this is not so of the early ones in which dragons are tamed and befriended. Here too perhaps we have a record of a changing attitude to paganism.

The Pagan mythic account has also been called into question.

Archaeology shows us that ancient pagan societies undertook large scale deforestation as they became agricultural societies (see Brown, 1997). There is also considerable debate about the role of ancient goddesses in feminism. On one hand it has been argued that the presence of female deities empowers women by allowing them to share in the divine nature, others have pointed out how often such deities are based on male stereotypes. Typically female deities are linked to fertility and perform the functions in the divine pantheon of wives and concubines in the world of humans, or perhaps one should say the world of men. The argument can thus be offered that far from liberating women, ancient goddesses were part of their dominance by men.

The relationship of paganism and Christian mission is also open for debate. There were different approaches ranging from those who saw God communicating in ancient paganism to those that saw it all as in some way demonic. In all cases Christianity came as a new faith that sought converts, but how this was done also varied. Possibly much early mission led to the adoption of pagan elements along with local culture within highly localised expressions of church. This is partly why the extent of the early church in places like China has been obscured as churches were so radically enculturated. In the West however, whilst early mission seems to have followed a similar pattern, the development of the Holy Roman Empire in 800 fused state and religion, making religious expansion part of military conquest and religious dissent an act of treason. This accompanied a gradual rejection of indigenous expressions of Christianity and more aggressive approaches to paganism. This marked a gradual shift from the rooting of Christianity in the context of local pagan sites and stories to their destruction and replacement. For instance, the Christian use of sacred wells in Britain and the adoption of pagan festivals preserved as positive much of the paganism encountered. This has had the interesting effect of being one of the ways paganism has been preserved and thus a source for those seeking to revive Paganism. This is in contrast with the destruction of pagan shrines by later Saxon missionaries like Boniface and the forced conversions of later missions to Baltic countries like Estonia. The incorporation of pagan elements in European Christianity can itself be interpreted in different ways by Christians. It is viewed by some, like myself, as a recognition of the positive contribution of pagan religion as the early missionaries encountered it. Others, however, have viewed it as a dangerous failure to fully Christianize (see Hollinghurst 2010. pp.112-152, Wessels 1994, Brown 2006 and Bosch 1993, pp.190–213).

How this history has been viewed by Pagans is also not agreed. Famously Margaret Murray's thesis that there was a continuous witch cult in Europe going back to pre-Christian religion held a lot of popular support, but has been roundly dismissed academically (see Hutton, 1991). Contemporary Paganism is now viewed by academics as a new religion, if one drawing inspiration from the little we know of ancient Northern European paganism. We have better records of paganism in the Middle East or ancient Greece, but even then it would be difficult to claim that contemporary followers of *Natib Qadish* or worship of Zeus in Greece are really following ancient faiths. None of this makes contemporary Paganism less valid or any less worthy of respect, but it does raise questions about the mythic histories of Pagans and Christians and how these two faiths relate to each other.

If contemporary Pagans are not survivors of an ancient tradition this also means they are not tarred with any of its potentially unsavoury elements. The same cannot be said for Christians who have to accept that in Christendom even when the myth is stripped away some of what is left is not good. This raises questions not only of why this happened, but also whether it could happen today. I think much of the problem was the alliance of faith and state, and with the dying of Christendom it may be this toxic mix will fade. But the church's past suggests it will be right to ask today's Christians about their attitude in a number of areas; to other religions and difference between people in general, to evangelism and conversion; to the environment and ecology; and on questions of power and gender. If contemporary Pagans have sought to embrace difference, live well with the planet and tackle ecological issues and promote flat power structures and gender equality they may fear Christians, judging by their history, will not.

Exploring different Christianities today

That Paganism is very diverse is well accepted. Even knowing that a Pagan follows a particular path will not enable you to properly understand that individual's own expression of their Paganism. By contrast there is a tendency, especially among its critics, to view Christianity as rather monolithic, assuming there is 'a Christian view' or 'a Christian way of living'. Some Christians also think this way and so that impression can be supported, but actually there are many different Christianities and understanding this is important in addressing those big questions our mythic history leaves us. Here again the experience of European Christendom has made it feel far more fixed than in reality it has been. Even then the Reformation, and subsequent divisions among every increasing Protestant denominations, shows us this is not the case. Examining the world church or the early church shows just how much variety there is. Christians however, will take different views of this diversity. Some will welcome it, others view it as at best a failure of unity or at worst as forms of heresy. This will come down to their basic view of church, but also crucially of culture and faith. How Christians understand these issues is likely to determine how they relate to Pagans and the world around them.

In Christian thinking about other faiths it is often suggested there is a division between exclusivist and inclusivist approaches. This might be expressed in the question 'who goes to heaven?' In the first view only Christians do, in the second everyone does. Such an approach is itself based on Christian assumptions and today is often supplement by a pluralist view in which there are many different paths. In trying to explore this and expand it I have used both mathematical set theory and pictures that embody these different approaches (Hollinghurst, 2010, pp.167-189). I also realised that the taxonomy I was producing related to a different one produced earlier by H. R. Niebuhr (1951). I offer my taxonomy below and seek to relate it to the questions posed by our mythic history in the hope this is helpful for Pagans seeking to relate to Christians today.

The Exclusivist approach can be viewed as a bounded set. A line is drawn dividing those who are inside it from those outside it. In the version known as double predestination Calvinism, God draws the line and chooses some and not others and there is nothing we can do about it. This is all about God's sovereignty and thus suggesting we might choose to cross the line and come in is to suggest God is not in control. However, most versions of this exclusivist approach have some concept of conversion in which people can be brought in. This leads to an image of church as a lifeboat or the Ark from the Noah story. This church then has a mission, to save people from drowning. This view tends to see the world 'out there' as corrupt and full of lost people who need saving from it. Other religions are likely to be viewed as at best misguided and at worst as demonic deceptions. As this indicates there are 'harder' and 'softer' versions of this paradigm. In the harder version the world will ultimately be destroyed on the day of judgement when those who are 'in' are taken up to heaven. However, there are Christians who take this basic approach, but believe in heaven coming on earth and so take a view in which those who are 'in' have a calling to bless the world outside that God wants to change and not simply save souls for heaven. Similarly there are those who would be more positive to God being at work 'out there', but if so that will largely be to help people come 'in'. The hard end of this view is of course very much like the picture of a witch hunting society given by Mary Douglas. Those who are in must keep themselves safe from the evil 'out there'. In various versions of this those 'out there' will also include a number of Christian groups deemed for one reason or another apostate. This view I believe relates to Niebuhr's 'Christ against culture' in which being Christian is viewed as counter-cultural and culture viewed as corrupt and corrupting.

One of the variances within this view is to do with the boundary. Is it infant baptism or adult baptism? Or saying a prayer of repentance? Or being accepted into church membership? Or being filled with the Holy Spirit? Disputes between exclusivists over this can be bitter; after all you are telling others they are not 'in' if they haven't crossed your version of the boundary. Other Christians have learned to live with these differences and seek common boundaries, but somewhere the boundary of orthodoxy will be drawn and there will be those outside it. One of the consequences of the decision in the West to make infant baptism the boundary around the time Christianity was being established as a state religion in Rome was that it became automatic to baptise all children and eventually forcibly baptise all citizens with few exceptions. The church boundary effectively became the state boundary. This eventually turned evangelism into conquest. It is also precisely under these conditions that things like the Inquisition arose to police those who didn't really want to be 'in'.

This is exactly what is feared in the Pagan mythic history, and at its hard end are Christians who see themselves as saved and going to heaven while Pagans and the planet are sent to burn in the flames of hell. However, the attitude of such Christians to inter-faith dialogue is like that of governments who won't talk to terrorists, so they are highly unlikely to be at such events. This doesn't stop them posting messages on the internet or picketing

Pagan events. At the soft end inter-faith dialogue may be welcomed, sometimes in the hope of converting people of other faiths, but often as part of a vision for a good society. Here though they are likely to prefer talking to Muslims and Jews than to Pagans. Bounded set people like to know where the boundaries are, so they may respond better to Pagans who they can easily identify and understand. This may be an anathema to Pagans who tend to like not being pigeonholed. One of the issues here is that inter-faith groups have often been a bounded set with various groups, including Pagans, on the outside. I have heard a lot of bounded set thinking from some in the inter-faith movement when Pagan membership is raised. 'If they come in how will we stop X joining?'; 'They need a body to represent them before they can join'; 'How do you define what a Pagan is anyway?' are all examples.

The Inclusivist approach is, by comparison, an open set; there are no boundaries and everyone is in. The image is of a God who loves all people and welcomes all people just as they are. In this view the church exists for all and wants to show God's love to all without seeing them as in need of conversion. In practice even 'hard' inclusivists will probably recognise that some people do need to change, but they are likely to think that offering 'bad people' love and acceptance is the best way to help them change. Open set Christians will be caring and likely to care about issues of justice and the environment. This approach I believe relates to Niebuhr's 'Christ of Culture'. This stresses the coming of God into the world in Jesus and has an incarnational vision in which local culture is affirmed.

Open set Christians often like inter-faith work and think Pagans should be included, because everyone should be. If this seems like the ideal sort of Christian there is a consequence of this approach that Pagans and others find annoying. The basic assumption is that all religions are really the same and differences between people or faiths are not relevant. Others can be assumed to be, using Karl Rahner's phrase, 'anonymous Christians'. This doesn't work for those who are clear they are not Christians and want to emphasise their own religious path. This desire to affirm faiths as different, but not excluded, leads to pluralist approaches to faith and culture. In this area, however, I think there are modernist and postmodernist approaches.

The Modernist Pluralist approach is a multi-set approach. In this view there are many different religions each with its own boundary, but all are viewed as equally valid. Each has its 'in and out', but all are welcomed. The Christian religion will be one of these, Paganism another along with many more. This approach is likely to advocate multi-faith events and things like the World Parliament of Religions. Other faiths are seen as different, but are affirmed. However, the modernist version has a twist. The story that best sums up the modernist pluralist approach is that of the blind men and the elephant. A version of this story can be found in ancient China about 2,000 years ago (and in the Theravada Buddhist Pali Canon, Udana vi.4, a few centuries earlier) but in the West it seems to have come into currency in the 19th century. The blind men each feel one part of the elephant, one concludes from the trunk it is a type of snake, another feels the tail concluding it is a rope, one feels the tusks and assumes it to be a type of spear, the next feels the side and concludes it's like a wall, and finally one feels the leg and decides it to be like a tree. The men then fall to arguing, each insisting their interpretation is correct. The Chinese version ends by making the point that one should not presume to pronounce on the nature of the whole until one knows the sum of all the parts. The later version by John Saxe in Linton's *Poetry of America* 1878, specifically applies the parable to theological argument; different understandings result from only seeing part of the whole. It has come in popular usage to mean that different religions are like the different perspectives of the blind men; each is true but only partial. All religions then lead to God, but none has all the answers. If all do lead to God, then the idea of seeking to convert someone from one religion to another makes no sense. Instead one enters into dialogue with other religions in order to learn more about the reality all religions are seeking to express.

However, the story has an interpretation that can be uncovered in the writings of those espousing this approach. The story relies on somebody telling it who can see the elephant, and in the end there are not really a whole series of different animals but one elephant. So in fact if all religions are partly true they are all also partly false. Indeed, if one could see it there is really one true religion just as there is one real elephant. This is I think reflected in a tendency amongst some advocates of religious pluralism to in effect place the template of the elephant across the world's religions and say on the one hand see how much the faiths have in common, yet at the same time bits outside the elephant's shape are dismissed as forms of unworthy cultural bias or religious exclusivism. In effect this approach puts a broad bounded set over the multiple sets and welcomes all faiths in it, but only in the areas they agree with the larger whole. I think this approach therefore relates to Niebuhr's 'Christ above culture' in which a superior Christian position can be taken, even though here it is a superior view that has moved on from Christian distinctiveness.

Comments made by John Hick in *The Myth of Christian Uniqueness* are revealing (2005, pp.30-34). He suggests that any notion of Christian uniqueness can be rejected by comparing its moral contribution to that of other faiths. All faiths, he argues, share the 'golden rule' of treating others as we would wish to be treated, but all have contributed negatively as well as positively to the good of the world. Significantly he judges what good is according to Western liberal moral standards. He therefore has to argue these are not products of the dominance of the Christian tradition in the West, but the enlightenment re-discovery of Greek thought. In effect, it could be argued that Hick believes all faiths can be judged from the 'superior' position of Western liberalism.

Because Christianity is not unique in Hick's judgement, he rejects the doctrine of the incarnation as God uniquely becoming human in Jesus as a creation of the early church alien to Jesus' own understanding. Instead he offers an 'inspirational' understanding of incarnation in which God can be incarnate in any person through inspiring them to good. He notes that such ideas will be opposed by those he refers to as 'creedal fundamentalists' (2005, p.32). However, by elevating Western liberalism to an objective position from which the world's faiths are judged and then replacing their traditional beliefs with re-interpretations that enable each to fit his position, all Hick does is remake Jesus, and other faiths, in his own likeness.

Similarly, Driver argues each religion can be judged by their work for the liberation of the poor and oppressed (2005, p.209); the basis of his 'super-religion'. Those like Hick and Driver take the part of the un-named narrator who sees the whole elephant and thus knows the blind men are only feeling bits of it. So the claim to affirm every religion masks the reality that some true 'super-religion' is assumed to exist by which all other religions can be judged.

However, not all pluralists think this way. Raimon Panikkar seems aware of the danger of creating a 'super-religion', arguing there is no objective place to judge religions. They must be recognised to occupy their own segregated worlds of understanding. We must, he argues, not seek a unified position, but one in which the faiths travel together in confidence (2005, p.103-109). In this he moves towards a more postmodern pluralism.

The Post-Modern Pluralist approach is in fact a pure multi-set approach with no added shape by which all faiths can be judged. As such there is no longer one elephant with different views but a whole set of different animals and each blind man is seeing part of a different one. Indeed with philosophical approaches that borrow from Nietzsche the denial of anything one could meaningfully call a 'real' world, it is simply not possible, as Pannikar argues, to judge anything true or false or indeed good or bad. I relate this to Niebuhr's 'Christ and Culture in Paradox'. This is not as good a fit, but has the idea within it of tensions that are to be left unresolved, which also features in the post-modern approach.

If the post-modern approach does affirm all religions as they are, it may yet leave another problem. How will they relate well to each other? This question also haunts post-modern culture, which on the one hand affirms difference but on the other offers no mechanism to prevent those differences fighting until one of them has beaten the others. In this sense whilst belief in a God that is bigger than creation and can thus act as a moral guide can lead to autocratic and intolerant expressions of what that God is supposedly teaching; it is hard to live with difference unless there is some arbiter seeking the welfare of all expressions of difference. This of course might be something all faiths can come to agree on, but this seems unlikely whilst some see others in a negative light.

The Transformational approach is the last one I wish to offer. There may well be others, but at present these five seem to cover the differences I have noted so far. This is a centred set approach. This shifts the question from, 'In or out?' to, 'Which direction are you going and how much further is there to go?' One analogy of this might be that of a sheep farmer in the Australian outback who keeps his flock together by sinking a well rather than building a fence knowing they will not stray from the source of water. In image terms this might also be like the picture of people ascending the same mountain by different paths. But there is a top to the mountain, which is a definite destination and one that all can head towards. However, unlike the elephant, you can't see the top till you get there and whilst you may as you get nearer the top start to see some of those on the other paths there may be some who emerge from the other side quite unexpectedly. There are different ways one can extrapolate this analogy. It may be that some paths are not as good as others. It might be that near the top the paths run out and climbers on each path need to help each other negotiate the bare rock. Near the top there may be only one path, which all have to join and which may or may not be one of the originals. Or all might reach the top by different routes.

There are some consequences of this image. As each path gets closer to the summit it also gets closer to the other paths, each is changed by the journey until ultimately each joins up on the summit. Different religious journeys are affirmed, but ultimately there is only one religious destination. Because no-one can yet see the top no-one can be sure their path is the right one. But perhaps as each traveller gets nearer to the top and thus nearer each other they will start to see patterns emerging between them that hint of where they are going. It might also be that there are messages of guidance and encouragement coming from the summit, something like the voices of religious teachers and scriptures. These are not heard clearly when we start our climb, but they become clearer as we reach the top, and will turn out not to be conflicting messages at all. It's just that we can't be sure yet what we have heard correctly and what we have misheard.

In the Christian version of this story Jesus has come down the mountain to tell us what it is like at the top and is now helping us climb if we wish it. I am inspired by Jesus' vision and helped by him to progress, but until I reach the top I can't be sure if I have heard Jesus correctly or properly understood him. So I have to be open to the discoveries I will make on the journey. In a Christian understanding the goal of the journey is twofold, to become the person I am meant to be by becoming Christ-like; and to enter what Jesus calls the Kingdom of God. This, however, is where the analogy breaks down because the Kingdom of God is not, as Jesus talks of it, a place I travel to, but a way of living that enters into this world and transforms it. The image here that

Jesus uses is of leaven in dough that makes the bread rise. This approach would relate to Niebuhr's image of 'Christ transforming culture'.

The image of the church offered by Jesus' story of the leaven is of cross-cultural explorers who in each place become indigenous and yet bring with them a vision of how each place could be better so they become agents for change from within. This is not, however, a pre-existing blueprint so everywhere becomes the same, rather each place has a unique way of being at its best that is only uncovered during the journey towards it. This journey can only be undertaken with the locals and can't be imposed upon them. This approach is that of the Catholic missionary Vincent Donovan as he writes:

> Do not try to call them back to where they were, and do not try to call them to where you are, beautiful as that place may seem to you. You must have the courage to go with them to a place neither you nor they have been before. (2001, preface)

This is a very different model of evangelism from the bounded set approach. Donovan's approach is akin to that which formed the highly indigenised churches of the East or indeed the Celtic church. The Celtic church was therefore as much a product of the Irish and Druidic as it was of the Romano-British Christians who came to Ireland as its founders. Such an approach today would see Christians and Pagans sharing their different vision of where we are going, but in doing so seeking to inspire each other as well as explore differences. Because this is a vision for how we live in the world it also has to address issues of justice and ecology. Indeed, the vision is of a transformed creation not of a heaven away from creation. Pagans and Christians may disagree on this; Pagans may well see creation as working perfectly well so only humans need to change. The Christian vision has always been of a changed world in which suffering and death ends.

What that actually may mean in practice clearly doesn't fit with the current laws of physics or biology. Indeed what divine ecology will finally look like is firmly out of sight at the top of the mountain.

Pagans and Christians sharing on the journey

If Pagans and Christians are going to move forward on a journey that leads to positive change in our society we need to shed some of the weight of our mythic histories. Pagans and Christians will also have to get to know each other better and accept the differences within each faith as well as those between them. This will mean that some Pagans and some Christians will find it much easier to get on than others. Those that do can also help each other with the more wary sections of our own faith communities.

At times of change Christianity tends to change, and at times of great change it changes greatly. This is often uncomfortable for Christians who may become defensive of their traditions often in opposition to those of other Christians. Aggressive expressions of Christianity are often really targeting other Christians. Pagans may find themselves caught in the cross-fire. We are at present going through a time of great change and there are many in the church radically re-thinking its future path. If we go down what I have referred to as a transformational route, then we will see expressions of church that are re-indigenised in our context. Some of these are quite likely to learn a lot from the Pagan community. Indeed this is part of the story of Forest Church (see chapter 9), which is seeking to re-connect Christianity with the land and, in the words of Graham Harvey, the non-human people we share it with (see Stanley and Hollinghurst, 2014 and Stanley, 2013). For some this will be about a re-indigenised Christianity that will learn from Paganism, but remain distinctly Christian. It is also clear that for some a form of Christo-Paganism is possible. I suspect that the question 'Who is Jesus?' will be crucial in determining where people find themselves with regards to

Christian/Pagan identity.

There are areas of difference and debate between Christians and Pagans. But also much that can be a shared vision for a good society. For Christians this is the Kingdom of God or I might today prefer the divine eco-system. I am not sure of a Pagan term for this, but have found this idea of the good human life with all creation very much part of Paganism, and one of the reasons I see Paganism as a really positive contribution in today's world.

The logic of much Christianity is that what God does in Jesus is good news for all, so many Christians will seek to invite Pagans to experience that. This is evangelism and its Christendom history has not been good. Pagans don't have an equivalent to the Christian notion of salvation, but can be pretty persuasive advocates of their own tradition. Indeed, I would suggest they are very good evangelists. Can this be done in a respectful way? Much of this will depend again on what kind of Christians and Pagans we are talking about. I think the centred set approach offers a far more ethical and humble background to faith sharing because it recognises Christians simply cannot claim to have all the answers and expects much to be learnt from other faiths. It also sees conversion as about changing our lives not a church recruitment drive. But even avowed exclusivists can work out that offending people only puts them off!

Christianity has often been patriarchal, but many Christians would now recognise and reject this, and Paganism has played some part in this. Most Christian theologians would recognise that the divine feminine should be as much a part of Christian faith as the divine masculine. Yet the church on the whole has not been good at putting this into its language. I hope here, too, Pagans can prompt Christians to realise that this is important. The same is true regarding the environment where Pagans have played a part in inspiring Christians in adopting environmentalist agendas.

The history of the encounter between Christians and pagans

has left us stories, images and places that record it. When we visit a saint's well or look at an image of St Brigid or hear the story of Arthur or George and the Dragon we are entering into the way our British Isles gives witness to that history. How do we read these? As a sign of Christians driving out Paganism? A sign of Christianity entering a Pagan context and adopting it whilst transforming it in something distinctive called Celtic Christianity? Or a sign of Paganism and Christianity as equals in harmony? We have lived for many centuries in 'Christian Britain' and so these stories' official versions have been Christian. We live now, however, in a post-Christendom society in which contemporary Pagans have every right to offer their interpretations of such places and stories. It is good for Christians to realise these are contested ground and that there are other ways of reading our history. Indeed, encountering contemporary Paganism can help Christians re-examine these stories and come to new understandings that help Christians fulfil a better role in today's world. It would be very easy for both communities to remain entrenched in their own mythic histories and make Britain's sacred landscape and tales a battleground between us. My hope is that instead we can move out of our mythic bunkers and share these spaces and stories and find that together we can enrich them and they enrich us.

Chapter 3

Fears and prejudices: A Pagan view

Graham Harvey

According to the bard William Blake, who both Christians and Pagans have claimed as their own (whether rightly or wrongly), 'Opposition is true friendship'. The tenor of Blake's *Marriage of Heaven and Hell* (in which this assertion is made just beneath his writhing image of Leviathan) is that life is made possible only by the existence of difference, oppositions and even conflicts. The sterility, entropy and boredom of complete agreement, unity or monoculture is an absolute threat to life. This is especially true if one option is forcibly imposed rather than welcomed.

Nonetheless, the proliferation of diversity and opposition bring difficulties as well as pleasures. On the same plate (20) of the *Marriage of Heaven and Hell*, Blake has an angel say, 'Thy phantasy has imposed upon me & thou oughtest to be ashamed.' This resonates with the purpose of my attempt to 'address our respective fears and prejudices' (the task given me) in as much as confronting falsehoods probably ought to help us to reject the fantasies we impose on others. But Blake's answer to the angel ('We impose on one another, & it is but lost time to converse with you whose works are only Analytics') reminds me that the word 'academic' commonly means 'irrelevant' today. Although I celebrate academia and the project of inspiring research (the habits of questioning and debating), I write here as an animist Pagan, frequent participant in Pagan ceremonies, and celebrant of life on planet earth. Hopefully, then, the respective 'fears and prejudices' which we raise, confront and address when we meet in dialogue or ceremony will be of more than analytical value and will aid us in efforts to celebrate our earth-home.

More positively, it is a fact worthy of considerable celebration that at least some Christians and some Pagans (and people from other religions or none) find the celebration of earth to be a valued common ground. Knowing that we have shared locations and horizons (actual and metaphorical), we can face fears and prejudices. We probably have shared journeys to take and shared relations with whom to dwell and travel. Anyway, our conversations together will be more likely to reach positive outcomes if we unburden ourselves both of fears and prejudices that create illusory barriers and of false unities that too quickly set aside our differences. Blake's 'opposition' which is 'true friendship' is not aggression, but clarity about ourselves and our others.

Thinking about who ee/you think you/we are

The title for the first session in the Ammerdown Conversation between Pagans and Christians was, 'Addressing our Respective Fears and Prejudices'. This invited participants to take a look in the murky shadows and see what some of our less enlightened fellow religionists think. In this chapter I note some of those perceptions, elaborating on just a few in a little more detail. Being a scholar of religion as well as a Pagan (who used to be a Christian and has a degree in Christian theology), I propose to summarise and challenge some of the clichés that can be asserted in what are, I argue (at more length elsewhere than I will do here), the less useful discussions of religion. I also direct attention towards some similarities between us all: e.g. those of our embodiment and those of our enculturation into capitalist modernism. In doing so, I will also suggest a brief incursion into the territory that the phrase 'Celebrating Planet Earth' (offered as the overarching title of our Ammerdown gathering) suggests to me about the common ground we already inhabit and may yet learn to celebrate more vibrantly.

In preparation for talking at Ammerdown I tried to think about what our fears and prejudices might be. That is, I pondered what Pagans think about Christianity and what Christians think about Paganism. I also wondered what might be understood when people hear the names of our religions. If I listed some of these alleged contrasts and clichés they would largely tell us about the views of people who are unlikely to be interested in respecting others. People who get involved in inter-faith dialogue tend to have fairly positive or hopeful views of others. But maybe this is naïve and, in reality, if we dig down we may find surprising fears or prejudices. We can deal with that by listening more carefully to one another. However, more challengingly, we might just find that we have misunderstood matters because we have imagined others to be almost like us but not quite. By that I mean that it is easy to think that other people mean what we would mean when they say or do things. In reality it is often the case that people use words to mean entirely different things, in which case we can find that we have been busy 'talking past each other'.

Before we go further, the never to be forgotten fact is that Christianity and Paganism are both immensely diverse. These terms label varied and ever-evolving experiments in being human, experiments in being one species in a multi-species world, and experiments in improving (to our satisfaction at least) whatever we mean by 'Christianity' and 'Paganism'. All the clichés, fears and prejudices about our chosen religious lifeways should be tested against that primary and foundational acknowledgement of diversity. One way to do this is to insist that phrases like 'Christianity teaches' or 'Paganism encourages' are ungrammatical. It is people who teach and encourage, not imaginary systems, fluid networks or assemblages of diverse participants. When we talk about what people do, rather than about what systems are alleged to do, we will keep diversity in clear view.

That would be a good start, but to belabour the point about keeping diversity in view, we need to remember that not everyone thinks or acts alike. This is one reason for being certain that any 'respective fears and prejudices' that we, Christians or Pagans (and others), might harbour are likely to be fantasies. We will better grasp the diversity and vitality involved here if we insist on talking about what particular Christians or particular Pagans think, say or do. Another facet of this same point is that Pagans do not like everything that other Pagans do. Christians do not like everything that other Christians do. One task for religious people in dialogue (of the kind that celebrates diversity and even opposition) is to resist and challenge the small visions and petty fantasies that are sometimes imposed on others. If we see those monstrous fantasy clichés more clearly, instead of having to issue angry denials we might become free to laugh together at mis-perceptions and mis-representations. If nothing else, humour might make our encounters and our world a better place.

Perceiving each other

Let me, nonetheless, set out what some of those fears, perceptions and clichés might be in a brief table of summary words or phrases. Some of these may be more blatantly false or skewed than others. Some of them may resemble your lived reality, experience or ambitions more than others. Remember that items that some people identify as negative will seem positive to others.

Christianity	Paganism
About obeying authoritative deity	About celebrating natural world
Authority in texts and hierarchies	Authority in individual now
Salvation	Enchantment
Revealed	Natural
Uninterested in earth	Encourages respect for earth

Focused on afterlives	Focused on present lives
Sees bodies as sinful	Encourages bodily celebration
Turns the teachings of Jesus into dogmas	Discourages dominating leadership styles
Patriarchal	Feminist
Respectable	Eccentric
Communal	Individualist
...	...

This isn't a complete list. Its incompleteness is hinted at by my leaving the last line marked only by dots. It does, though, set out some of the stuff that the media and our wider society appear to assume about us. Many other lines could be added and filled in.

Each item in each column could be the subject of lengthy discussion. (Is it really true that Christian leaders privilege groups over individuals? Is it really true that Paganism has been profoundly shaped by Feminism?) Then we could start again, discussing to what degree the two columns work as contrasts. (Are there more eccentrics among Pagans than among Christians? Do Christians really rely more on what they read than on what they see among their friends?) In doing so, we might learn some things about both Christianity and Paganism, or about how some people perceive these religions, or about how different emphases and contrasts are employed. Certainly we would need to seek nuances and alternatives in each case. We might want to suggest that some of the seeming contrasts offer a continuum along which both Christians and Pagans may find themselves pushed and pulled, attracted and repelled.

We might also want to turn the tables in some cases. For example, it might be that some Pagans turn the teachings of Jesus into dogmas more than some Christians do. It is certainly common for people to use 'what Jesus taught' or 'what Jesus was like' as a standard against which to judge what Christians are alleged to think or to be like. It is equally common to find that Pagans and others stereotype Jesus as a 'nice man' and 'good teacher' while Christians are perfectly able to cite examples of Jesus being aggressive towards his contemporaries and maybe to most of humanity in the future. My point here is not to fix on any one of these views of Jesus, Christianity or Paganism, but to invite consideration of the perceptions and prejudices that can affect encounters between people.

Essences and essentialisms

In a number of the less useful books about religions, people have conned themselves into thinking that they have found one word with which to categorise whole religions or batches of religions. I used one example in the above table, i.e. in the contrast between 'revealed' and 'natural' religions. There is some truth in the idea that Christians talk more about revelation than most Pagans do. It is also true that most Pagans talk more about 'nature' than most Christians do. Or, to be more precise, these are topics that crop up in Christian and Pagan conversations or talks. However, it is absolutely facile to turn these bland statements into summaries of whole religions or into categorical distinctions between them. There are, for example, Pagans who regularly seek to be open and receptive to revelations from deities, ancestors, trees, rocks or hedgehogs. Indeed, ceremonies that create opportunities in which this might happen are central and perhaps even definitive of Wiccan Paganism. Elsewhere I have claimed that Paganism is not a 'spiritual path' but a 'sitting among the trees' (Harvey 2007, pp.137-8, 218). This deliberately playful claim was not meant to suggest that Pagans do not need to learn something or change in some way. Rather, I intended to suggest that many Pagans seek to learn 'that which is' or the way of the larger-than-human world. They celebrate the plain fact that we are already at home and now it is time to behave ecologically (at-home-ly in earth or bioregions perhaps). However, in thinking about the claim that Paganism is somehow 'natural' or 'about nature', we must acknowledge that there are also Pagans who experience the 'natural world' not as a place in which to honour other-than-human lives, but primarily as a source of inspiration for their individual personal growth, self-improvement or personal gnosis. If Paganism is a 'nature religion' to such Pagans, it is not (necessarily) an environmentalist one. I could expand on these challenges to my table's clichés, but I want to play with what is, to me, a somewhat more satisfactory 'essence'.

What I want to say might make more sense if I note a little more about how the 'essences' game has been played. It has been asserted that Christianity is essentially about 'salvation', Judaism about 'sanctification' and Buddhism about 'enlightenment'. There is some truth in these claims. They point to central facets of these religious complexes, providing single word indicators of the kind of thing Christians, Jews or Buddhists talk to each other about. They might also summarise the kind of thing that such people differ with each other about. That is, it might be that there are different kinds of Christianity because of differences of opinion over the means and processes of salvation. There are different kinds of Judaism because people differ over the degree to which observance of particular food rules is required in a sanctified life or community. There are different kinds of Buddhism because people differ about the processes involved in achieving or promoting enlightenment. And so on. These are not sufficient ways of telling the story of Buddhism, Christianity or Judaism – let alone telling the story of the diversity of Buddhist, Christian and Jewish lives. They have a limited utility and require careful treatment. Nonetheless, let's see what happens if we pursue the idea of essences to seek better ways to understand relations between Pagans and Christians.

So, accepting for now that Christianity might be about salvation, is there a single word for what Paganism is about? In my table of perceptions earlier in this chapter, I already gave the game away and contrasted Christian 'salvation' with Pagan 'enchantment'. Here's a little evidence for the value of that: many Pagans are ex-Christians. Some of us can be as wrapped up in what is wrong with Christianity as ex-smokers or ex-coffee drinkers can be about what is wrong with their past obsessions or addictions. Like such people, most ex-Christian Pagans usually get through that and can then judge their past as a part of becoming who they are now, a part that does not require continuous rehearsal or recrimination. Often, however, the thing that stands out when ex-Christian Pagans talk about their Christian experience is the idea that Christianity is about salvation from sin. Sometimes this is phrased along the lines that their break with Christianity only came when they rejected guilt and all that goes with it. (What 'goes with' guilt are not only feelings and confessions, but also notions about a deity who might seem to be obsessive about surveillance.) It is similarly true that ex-Pagan Christians often identify salvation from sin as the thing that Paganism lacks. Some say that they found themselves 'at home' in Christianity when they realised their need for help and that Pagan deities are rarely interested in such matters. For some ex-Pagan Christians the very notion of having dealings with Pagan deities is the primary thing they cite as requiring salvation. For some, the core of the 'good news' claimed by Christianity is that there is an alternative to 'nature' that is worth proclaiming. (In some classical theologies, the problem of 'nature' is particularly a problem of 'the body', or bodily needs and desires. Care is needed here as many Christian teachers have struggled to counter the temptation towards a dualistic separation of 'body' and 'spirit' that others have found in these metaphors of embodiment.) There again, there are people who blend Christianity and Paganism. Matters might be different for many of them. Perhaps they might feel that one religion offers salvation from sin while the other offers something else. That something might be enchantment.

Enchantment and modernity

One way to think about enchantment and disenchantment is to contemplate images that might purport to show us where we live. In talks and books about ecology or 'gaia' it is almost the default position to use a photo taken from Apollo 17 of our small, dynamic, beautiful, but fragile, planet with a backdrop of empty darkness or alien stars. I am not alone in thinking that this really is not a good way to represent our reality. It encourages the thought that we humans can gain an all-seeing view. It can suggest that we have or might gain an ability to manage the world. Management is a defining characteristic of modernity, an ideological system rooted in increased bureaucracy, seeking ever-more efficient bureaucratic and technological solutions to problems. Order and control over messy reality are inherent. The prognosis for the subjects of modernisation is further alienation and depersonalisation. But there is good news (at least, I think this is good news): according to Bruno Latour (1993), 'we have never been modern'. Although we have tried to be modern, and bureaucrats and technocrats have tried even harder to modernise everyone and everything, modernity does not and cannot work. Too many facets of reality are too messy, slippery and tricky to be systematised and routinised.

More importantly, the neat categories of modernity do not and cannot work because stuff keeps mixing up. Prime and relevant examples can be found in the ideas of nature and culture. These might seem to label distinct and different domains: 'culture' is what humans do, and varies from place to place, community to community, such that it becomes 'cultures', while 'nature' is the background scenery or stage in which human culture happens. 'Nature' is a single material realm, subject to rules that are easier to identify than cultural norms and values. We humans visit nature, especially in the countryside or wilderness – but nature sometimes visits us as storms, floods, earth-slides and hungry tigers. It is easy to say these things, and they are implicit in the idea that Paganism is a 'nature religion' and the idea that 'the environment' needs protecting. They are equally implicit in the way in which universities keep the 'natural' and 'social' sciences in separate buildings. But the nature/culture distinction is a fiction that we should outgrow and overcome. Global climate change provides a good example of the hybrid fusion of the allegedly separate 'nature' and 'culture'. It is neither 'natural' nor 'human artefact' in any pure sense, but that is because the 'pure sense' is a fiction. You could say that it is both 'natural' and 'human artefact' and so try to reclaim these terms and their relations more positively. But in reality, when we face such dangers as climate change, fictions are best challenged.

Nearer to home, those who seek to engage with other-than-human beings often consider it necessary to leave human-dominated urban locations to go find 'nature' in the countryside or wilderness. These, too, are fictions that do not enable us to engage with the real world. It would be banal simply to observe here that the fields, hedgerows, woodlands and streams that make up 'the countryside' are not only the result of millennia of human (and other-than-human) labour. Even pointing out that 'wilderness' areas are almost entirely the result of forcible acts of removal of humans and of the 'wrong trees' or the 'wrong wolves' misdirects us towards big dramas. Closer to home and at an everyday scale, agricultural practices during the past century have rendered much of the countryside almost lifeless. Fields, in particular, are often monocultural, producing single species of grain. In contrast, the carpets in our homes are frequently vibrant ecosystems of minibeasts and microbeasts of many kinds. 'Nature' (if this refers to the diversity of other-than-human species and their interactions) is, therefore, easier to encounter in your home than in any agro-industrial wheat field.

If 'nature' does mean a multispecies community, we do not even need to get down to carpet level to find it. In the crook of the elbows (antecubital spaces) of each and every one of us there is a thriving community of lively bacteria. In a *New York Times* article, Nicholas Wade (2008) reported on research published in *Genome Research* about six groups of bacteria (Wade says 'tribes', the original article says 'divisions') living in human and mouse elbow crooks. Most of us are also familiar with the fact that our digestive systems are not only home to many 'good bacteria', but only work because those bacteria busily make nutrients available for absorption. Whatever else this might mean, it shows that each human (and mouse) is already a multispecies community, ecosystem, symbiont or inherently and inescapably relational being. Even on your most lonely day, 'you' are already a plural rather than single person. You can never really be alone. You do not need to leave your home to find other beings. You are already among them and they are among you.

This excursion among wheat fields and elbow crooks may justify the claim that 'nature' is an unhelpful word, pretending to point to a reality separate from humanity and human culture. But before we declare it redundant or abolished, we might briefly consider its putative opposite, 'culture'. If there is no 'nature' is there 'culture'? In writing about new ways of thinking about 'religion' (looking away from 'belief in spirits' to observe etiquettes of inter-species relationships), I have sampled a little of the growing research about cultural activities among animals, birds and plants (Harvey 2013, pp.77-98, 215). Many species observably do things that we typically label with the word 'culture'. Chimpanzees and crows use tools, earthworms decorate their burrows, dogs play tricks, and trees warn each other of approaching predators. We could simply extend our use of the word 'culture' to include acts by other-than-human species, groups and individuals who are currently subsumed within our 'nature' category.

There again, the long trajectory of disquiet about 'bodies' and 'natural desires' in many religions might encourage us to think that much of human 'culture' is in fact 'nature'. Some have proposed that we need to fuse these two difficult words in order to say something more truly descriptive of our world of 'nature-culture' or 'culture-nature'. I am, to be honest, not overly concerned to solve a conundrum that might not bother many other people. I certainly do not intend to make it more difficult to speak the English language! Rather, my point in spending time with these matters of the nature of the world and of humans is to indicate alternatives to the disenchantment proposed by modernity. The point is that modernity tries to re-make us and all our relations as cogs in a neatly organised, regular and machine-like system, replete with secure boundaries and divisions. Paganism is one mode of resistance to the processes that would separate, dehumanise, depersonalise and individualise us. Pagans are experimenting with ways of relating with the wider, larger-than-human world in which we do not seek dominance or control, but partnership, co-operation, mutual aid and co-responsibility among our relations (all other living beings).

If the 'gaia' earth-from-space picture illustrates modernist separatism and managerialism, how might we illustrate a more enchanted, Pagan view of reality? Until the news spreads that our elbow crooks are ecosystems, it is unlikely that a photo of such body parts will achieve iconic status. I propose, however, that we already have healthier images of the effort to live as members of a multi-species community. These are the myriad photos posted daily in social media of favourite places. A particular wood, hill, river, coast or mountain – or even a specific tree or rock – illustrates our affectionate relations with places. They demonstrate our belonging and the stages of our journeys among other persons (most of whom are not human). Even our pictures of cute animals can illustrate our symbiotic engagement with earthly others. Perhaps photos of memorials and gravestones for the dead also illustrate an enchanted world in which even those who have died are not separated from us. By establishing memorials we continue to resist the effort initiated by early modern (initially

Protestant) elites to educate us away from 'meaningless rituals' and 'communion with the departed'. In short, a wide range of photos of ordinary and/or dramatic engagements with other kinds of persons illustrate our belonging in networks of relations.

Paganism, at any rate, provides some examples of resistance to modernity and of the continuity of enchantment. This is not to say that Christians do not deserve recognition for similar efforts. My point is, rather, to elaborate on the thought that if 'salvation' is a useful term for summing up much of what is important within Christianity (including matters that Christians fight each other about) so 'enchantment' might have similar currency as a way of thinking about Paganism. I find it almost impossible to think of a thoroughly Pagan use for words related to 'salvation' (except, perhaps, among those Pagans who want to 'save the earth' or 'save the whales', but those are not quite the same thing really). Conversely, I find it quite straightforward to think of ways in which some Christians continue to value and increase enchantment against the ravages of modernity's alienating disenchantment. These may not be central and definitive of any particular kind of Christianity, but with the ongoing 'greening' of religions it is not difficult to find examples of Christians who celebrate the lives and wellbeing of other-than-humans *for their own sake* (rather than as metaphors or lessons for humanity). The tendencies towards polytheism and animism within Paganism may, however, make this easier. Here (to paraphrase Rorty 1998, pp.23-4) there is no encouragement of the thought that anyone (even deities) will make sense of it all, get it organised, sort out all the difficulties and lead us into a unified and harmonious future. There is, instead, the messy here and now that promises yet more exuberant proliferation of alternatives and challenges. Salvation is not on the cards, enchantment with occasional bewilderment is a more reasonable expectation.

Ecology and economy

My final thought, here, is to emphasise that while we may be different as Pagans and Christians, we are similar in being human. Our chosen or inherited ideas and activities may be different, but we are not alien species. Apart from all the other ways in which we are similar (e.g. in hosting similar bacterial communities and religious histories) we are deeply impacted by the current struggle between economy and ecology. Our political leaders seemed obsessed with solving economic problems and in treating these as if they were 'natural' – speaking of 'market forces' as if these were like the weather rather than like engineered or military activities. They talk about environmental issues as if they mean to do something one day, once the banking or housing 'crisis' is solved. More often, they place the burden of doing something on individuals (repeating the Pythonesque mantra 'you are all individuals') to mask the fact that there are no individuals, but only relations, kin, co-dwellers in communities made up of many co-evolving, mutually dependent species. They forget or ignore the fact that both 'ecology' and 'economy' refer to being 'at home'. The study and management of 'households' are interlinked: human homes and families being elements of larger networks of relations within localities and regions. As protest placards have declared (but more succinctly), ecological disaster would make economic security pointless. But we need more than speeches, more than slogans or manifestos, more than declarations and creeds to motivate, inspire or provoke us.

The common ground on which Pagans, Christians and all other people meet, whether to discuss celebrations or differences, is that of an ecology. Even those Christians who believe themselves to be passing through the earth en route to a more permanent and better place are, for now, dwelling here. They are not entirely divorced from those of us who consider ourselves to be already at home in the only place that will ever nourish and be nourished by us. At any rate, it is my view that in order for there to be a good future for any of the species that have evolved here in earth until now, we must see ourselves present in places and moments, touching and touched by other lives. One of the things religions might be about (because I don't think they really are about strange beliefs about unscientific stuff) is performing rituals that strengthen our relations with our other-than-human neighbours. Asked what animals 'get back from us' for all the uses we make of them ('eating them, singing about them, drawing them, riding them, and dreaming about them'), the Buddhist environmentalist Gary Snyder replied:

> An excellent question, directly on the point of etiquette and propriety, and putting it from the animals' side. The Ainu say that the deer, salmon, and bear like our music and are fascinated by our languages. So we sing to the fish or the game, speak words to them, say grace. Periodically, we dance for them. A song for your supper: performance is currency in the deep world's gift economy. (1990, p.75)

This is the economy our real position in the ecological ebb and flow of things requires of us. To paraphrase leading ritual studies expert Ronald Grimes' (2013) jazz-like riff on Snyder's work, after hundreds of years of cultured disdain for ritual, we must re-learn ways of performing that will place us back among the webs of relations of earth-dwelling beings. We must demonstrate our belonging and our efforts to enhance the diversity of life. Talking and writing statements will not be enough although talking together (like eating together and walking together) are excellent ways to commit to better friendships. We need to be in the world as full participants (not as lords, stewards, managers or technocrats) in the household of related beings, refreshing the world by joining in multi-species rituals of gift giving and receiving.

Section

B

Possibilities for co-operation

Chapter 4

Building on ancient roots: Paganism and Christian paths

Liz Williams

Why are so many people in contemporary Western society drawn to the affiliation of different paths known as 'paganism'? This form of spirituality is growing, its demographic changing; it is becoming increasingly acceptable and mainstream. But what is 'paganism'? Where does it come from, and are we right in claiming ancient roots for this very modern form of spirituality?

History

Most people, including many contemporary pagans, will say that the kinds of spirituality that fall under the umbrella of paganism are 'ancient'. Druidry, witchcraft and shamanism are seen as being old practices, indigenous to the islands of Britain. To an extent, of course, this is true. Roman writers such as Tacitus commented on the Celtic tribal priesthood of the Druids; on their learning and lore. But since the Celts were a purely verbal culture, we don't know very much about what the Druids actually *did*; all we know of their practices comes from Roman writings, which may not be reliable. Colonial powers rarely report with accuracy on the peoples they have conquered: sometimes portraying them as mere peasants, in contrast to the sophisticated oppressor, sometimes as barely-human fiends, to highlight the bravery of 'our' soldiers in going to war against them. Roman writings on the Celts may be little more than propaganda, or early tabloid sensationalism for the folks back home.

Whereas we know relatively little about the Celts, we know rather more about Saxon and Viking practices, which are rather better documented. And we also have a reasonable idea about later British witchcraft – Medieval grimoires and pamphlets of spells give us some conceptual understanding of the kind of magic that people were practising from the Norman Conquest onwards. Here, the invention of the printing press, in particular, is our friend as historians of magic. And from its output, we can see that the magical practices of these islands were similar to indigenous practices throughout the world: relating to healing, cursing, love and money spells, magical work to protect animals and crops. Most of it came out of the Christian tradition. Britain was Christianised early, and despite the wishful thinking of some modern Pagans, little remained of Saxon or Celtic religions in terms of either theology or practice – there is little or no evidence for any secret cults worshipping ancient deities continuing into Medieval times, although some superstitions and herb lore may have continued from earlier practices. But people describing themselves as cunning folk, or those who were described as witches, would have had a primarily Christian theological underpinning, believing in God, Christ, angels and demons. Grimoires such as the 17th century Goetia are all about summoning demons to do your bidding – then invoking angels if the demons get out of hand! Charms to call on the powers of the saints were popular, but references to any pagan gods were tangential at best, and usually involve cases where a saint, such as St Bridget, may have taken on the aspect of an earlier deity. Vestiges of any very early practices are thus thoroughly Christianised, although this did not, of course, mean that the Church approved of them.

Thus Christianity and historical witchcraft share a heritage; the practices that we find throughout British folklore owe little to the beliefs of our distant pagan ancestors, and we would be disingenuous were we to claim them as pagan. However, the great late 19th century occult societies, such as the Golden Dawn, emerged less from folk witchcraft and more out of Renaissance magical practice and esoteric systems such as Rosicrucianism. Many of the 20th century groups – Wicca and Druidry are two examples – have their roots in the Golden Dawn, and well-known practitioners such as Dion Fortune and Aleister Crowley were among its members. Its practices, which are well documented, were highly eclectic; an amalgam of Christian and Pagan, with deities such as Christ and Isis among those invoked. It is not really until the advent of Gerald Gardner and his system of Wicca that the esoteric in Britain begins to dispense with Christian precepts and moves on to something that we may refer to as predominantly pagan.

One of the most influential people in the course of 20th century magical practice, Gardner was the son of a timber merchant. Born in 1884, Gardner was asthmatic as a child and received no formal education. His governess took him abroad for the sake of his health, thus the young Gerald gained a wide experience of the world at a young age, and when he was at an age to do so, headed out for the Far East where he became a rubber and tea planter. His first few decades were spent in Malaysia and India, with intermittent visits back to Britain, until he retired. With his wife, Donna, Gardner returned to London and subsequently bought a house in the New Forest. Here, he was to meet a group of people who would change the course of his life.

They were known as the Crotona Fellowship, a primarily Rosicrucian group. Gardner, who'd had a lifelong interest in magical practice, claimed that some of the group had associations with a local coven, a form of witchcraft that had endured for hundreds of years. It is by no means clear this was the case: Gardner was likely to have been exaggerating, or perhaps someone was having a joke at his expense. Elements of what became Wiccan practice do have older roots, but mainly through the kind of folklore-based practices that we have briefly addressed above.

One of the Crotona Fellowship was a woman named Edith

Woodford-Grimes, a pillar of the local community, who assisted Gerald in drawing up a modern form of witchcraft – what was to become modern Wicca. Author Philip Heselton has done a comprehensive job in researching the roots of Wiccan practice, which come from the Golden Dawn, the writings of Aleister Crowley, British folklore, Gardner's own enthusiasms (which included naturism), and possibly more curious origins such as variations on the Scout movement and contemporary children's literature. Gardner was, from the accounts of those who knew him, an endearingly enthusiastic man, and with the help of various women friends – such as Edith herself and Doreen Valiente – penned a number of the texts and rituals that we associate with Wiccan practice. Gardner was often mischievous, and somewhat prone to romanticising the truth, so some of his claims about witchcraft need to be taken with a pinch of salt!

He became friendly with a number of people on the emerging occult scene, including the founder of the modern Order of Bards, Ovates and Druids, Ross Nichols. Druidry itself is obviously ancient, but its contemporary form owes relatively little to older practices, for reasons we have examined. In its modern variation, it emerges out of the 18th century network of gentlemen's clubs and a growing interest in history. An initial group was formed in 1717, and enthusiasm for druidry as a concept continued to wax and wane over the next couple of hundred years, gaining ground again during the heyday of the Golden Dawn, when William Butler Yeats, a member of that order, contributed so greatly to the revival of the so-called Celtic Twilight. Since then Druidry, initially a primarily Christian-based movement, has become increasingly pagan; looking back to the myths and legends of the Celtic nations for its spiritual material.

But the principal focus of Druidry was not, initially, theistic. It is Gardner who enthusiastically took up the notion of the God and Goddess, the Lord and Lady, as the polarities around which

Wicca is based. This male god is emphatically not the god of the Christians, being based on the Great God Pan who features in Victorian and Edwardian literature; in the works of Arthur Machen (e.g. 1894) and Kenneth Grahame (e.g. 1908), and it is here that we really begin to see alternative god-forms take root in what is described by historian Ronald Hutton (in his work *The Triumph of the Moon*) as, 'The only religion that England has ever given the world' (1999, p.vii). But who do Wiccans worship? Let's now take a look at the principal deities of Wicca.

The Goddess

Many Pagans simply worship deities known as the God and Goddess, who might take many names, or none. The Goddess herself is often said to have a triple aspect: three figures in one – the Maiden, the Mother and the Crone. There is not a great deal of evidence that our witch and cunning folk ancestors worshipped any goddess, certainly not one in this triple form: mainly, this derives from Robert Graves' famous work *The White Goddess* (1948), which is one of the first books to posit the Goddess in this kind of threefold manifestation. However, many of the ancient goddesses had more than one aspect – Hecate, for instance. This may be because as tribes intermingled, inter-married and took one another over, their deities merged and mingled also, in an enforced or organic syncretism.

However, regardless of where this threefold image comes from, it is a powerful and evocative image, which has proved to have resonance with many modern Pagans. It is linked with the symbol of the triple moon, which represents the new moon (maiden), full moon (mother) and waning moon (crone).

Some pagans also link the Goddess with the Earth herself, with Gaia. Others prefer to worship her as a moon goddess, Diana – the 'traditional' goddess of the witches. The Italian witch deity Aradia is also invoked, gaining popularity at the end of the 19th century with American folklorist Charles Leland's work

Aradia, or the *Gospel of the Witches* (1899). Pre-empting Gardner, Leland claimed that the novel is based on fact: citing groups of pagan covens in Tuscany, but like Gardner, it is probable that Leland was drawing more on romance than veracity.

The God

The male deity who is most commonly worshipped in witchcraft is known as Herne, or Cernunnos, or the Horned God. His image is sometimes confused with the image of the Christian devil, with his antlers and cloven hoofs. But this entity is not connected to Satan – images of the devil most probably come from the representations of the horned deity Baphomet, famously illustrated as a Sabbatic Goat by 19th century occultist Eliphas Levi, who is still revered today by some members of the Pagan community.

So where does the Horned God come from? His image is found in very early times, on the Gundestrap cauldron. Here, he is antlered and carries two snakes in each hand. Yet we do not really know who this figure is. He might be a human shaman, or perhaps even a representation of Hercules, who as a child kills two serpents who invade his cradle. The Horned God is also found as the Greek god Pan, whose goatish appearance and mischievous – sometimes dangerous – personality may contribute to later interpretations of Satan. The priestesses of Thessaly were said to have worshipped Pan, held to be a secret, wild lover of the moon goddess Diana.

Doreen Valiente (a friend of Gerald Gardner) points out that there are many images of horned gods throughout Buddhist and early Tibetan mythology, and it is possible that these made their way across to Europe over the centuries. Some people also cite cave paintings of an apparent shaman as evidence of a very early horned god, but the original painting has been somewhat modified in subsequent reproductions of it and it is necessary to be a little careful in making assumptions.

The name 'Herne' first appears as a 14th century huntsman in Windsor Forest, who offers his soul to the Devil if he can bag a certain number of deer. The Devil honours the bargain and Herne's horned ghost is said to be still seen in the Great Park at Windsor. He appears in Shakespeare's *The Merry Wives of Windsor* and later appears as a character in a 19th century novel by William Harrison Ainsworth (1943), which is where his modern incarnation comes from. So he is not exactly an ancient Celtic figure – but, like Aradia, comes in his current form from a colourful novel. Although he and Cernunnos have been conflated, the worship of the latter seems to have been centred around Paris, whereas Herne is a figure who is very much local to Berkshire. It has been suggested that the name 'Herne' comes from the old Saxon god Woden, who was also called Herian, after his role as the leader of dead souls, the Einheriar, and of the Wild Hunt.

Today, in many Wiccan covens, he is seen as the consort of the Goddess. He is her mate, and he is a god in his own right, of the greenwood, of animals, and of the natural world. In earlier days, witchcraft was regarded as a fertility cult, and the God is a highly sexual entity, much called-upon at Beltane! Representations of the God and Goddess, whatever form they may take, tend to be heteronormative and often more than somewhat stereotypical in terms of their gender-based attributes.

But these deities, in their various forms, are only a few examples of the god-forms worshipped within contemporary Wicca. Paganism is a broad path, and entities from a wide variety of traditions, primarily those of Europe and the Near East, are called upon. We have noted that the Egyptian pantheon played a role in the practices of the Golden Dawn, and throughout the 20th century, ceremonial magic – formal, highly ritualised and rule-governed – continues to invoke Egyptian gods and goddesses. Much of pagan practice, however, relies upon the deities of one's own ancestors, so those of Celtic extraction, for instance, may prefer to worship a range of Welsh, Irish or Scots deities or spirits. It is part of the eclectic character of modern Paganism that a number of these – such as the Welsh enchanter Gwydion – were not originally gods at all, but heroes or heroines of the great Welsh imaginative work, *The Mabinogion*. Paganism adopts a swashbuckling approach to theology, taking on archetypes and god-forms, transforming heroes into deities, reclaiming saints, ignoring gods whom we know from what little evidence there is to have been important to our ancient ancestors (I know no-one who worships the Celtic thunder god Taranis these days), changing the nature of deities entirely. There is a goddess group in Glastonbury who revere Rhiannon as a goddess of love and sex: originally, she was simply an otherworldly figure and her journey is one of sacrifice and abuse, but she has been revised by her worshippers. In a sense, these examples of transformation and syncretism are no more than modern instances of practices which have been commonplace throughout history: the Greek Hermes syncretised with Egyptian Thoth to form the composite Hermes-Trismegistus, who resurfaces in British alchemy as the pseudonymous originator of Hermeticism.

This do-it-yourself approach to theology is, of course, part of the post-modern appeal of Paganism. We noted at the beginning of this chapter that Paganism is becoming increasingly popular, with several thousand self-described Pagans appearing on the last UK census. The rise of Paganism in Britain and elsewhere is partly a reaction to the Christian church: the most devout Pagans are often those who have had a Christian upbringing. But it is also a reaction to rigidity and control: its tolerance of belief systems is appealing to those who do not adhere to the notion of one true path. Pagans argue all the time, but one of the arguments that is conspicuous by its absence is the claim that one's own god/dess – Odin, Athene, the Dagda – is the only true deity. I have never heard a Pagan claim that another worshipper's pagan god is non-existent, almost as though there is a relativistic, but tacit, agreement that this aspect of our loose theology is out of bounds.

Paganism is pantheistic and individualistic; preferring not to engage with differences of deity, although there is plenty of debate about doctrinal minutiae within Wiccan practice – thus bearing out the suspicion that a tendency to schism is the true commonality between all religions. Nor is Paganism a text-based religion: ancient texts, such as the Hermetic texts or the various grimoires, may be referenced, but are not treated as 'gospel'. The closest thing Wicca has to a dominant text is Gardner's *Book of Shadows* – a notebook, in other words, of litanies and thoughts. But despite attempts by more literal-minded Wiccan practitioners to turn this into some manner of sacred text, most Pagans remain resistant, preferring to rely on their own intuitions and insights than those received from a prevailing work or a hierarchical priesthood. Trying to organise Pagans is often frivolously, but accurately, compared to herding cats, and thus far the practices that fall beneath the broad canopy of its umbrella have resisted, in the main, any great degree of formal organisation.

There are other aspects which unite us, as Pagans. Many forms of Pagan practice are nature based, our festivals relying on the pattern of the seasons. Despite the possible etymological origins of the word – the Latin 'paganus' means 'country-dweller' – a large number of Pagans today live in towns and cities, divorced from the cycle of the agricultural year and the cycles of the moon. This form of spirituality is a way of reconnecting with the world around us, and Paganism's strong connection with environmental movements is also part of this 'back to nature' appeal. One hears a lot of Pagans say that when they discover the various paths of this spirituality, there is a feeling of 'coming home,' which may be due to a return to the perceived magic of the world experienced in childhood and may also, I think, be due to popular works of fantasy read when one was a child: the links between fantasy literature and Paganism are quite strong and bear further investigation.

Community also has a lot to do with this appeal: Pagans tend to fall into a number of demographics (science fiction and fantasy, environmentalism, role playing games, and folk music are often shared interests in the Pagan community) and finding like-minded people is a goal of many individuals. What Pagans have in common is generally evident – but what about Pagans and Christians?

Pagan and Christian: finding common ground

Where might Pagans and Christians find commonality, therefore? At first sight, these spiritual paths would seem to run in parallel with a degree of opposition. Fundamentalist Christians tend to be wary of Pagans, regarding Paganism, incorrectly, as a form of Satanic practice. Whilst Satanists do exist, no-one outside fundamentalist sects tend to regard them as Pagan, and they do not describe themselves as such. That wariness is mutual: many Pagans react strongly against fundamentalist forms of Christianity, viewing it as a threat (this is perhaps more prevalent in the USA, a much less secular society than the UK). But this dual antagonism is beginning to change, a transition emerging from both sides: inter-faith initiatives by groups such as the Pagan Federation, and outreach by Christian groups or individuals seeking to understand Paganism's growing popularity. In the course of these conversations, a form of common ground is starting to emerge, and I would suggest that it is taking a number of forms.

1. Shared roots in multi-contested space: both Christians and Pagans have the landscape of Britain in common. An obvious example is Glastonbury Tor, possibly the new Jerusalem of William Blake, which shares both legends of Joseph of Arimathea and (more recently) goddess worship. The sacred wells of Derbyshire and the Malverns are

dressed by both Christians and Pagans; in Ireland, certain trees are honoured by both Catholics and Pagan residents.

2. Belief in the principle of deity, regardless of content. In my *Guardian* column on contemporary Paganism, it has become clear that opposition lies – at least in the narrow confines of the comments thread – not between Pagan and Christian, but between people of faith and the 'new atheism', which often manifests as a form of fundamentalism. Even when I'm talking about witchcraft, the Christian commentators are invariably respectful; not so the New Rationalist followers of Richard Dawkins!

3. A sense of shared community. The Church has always had a social conscience; Paganism, being essentially a new religion, has hitherto been too introspective to follow suit, but this is starting to change. Glastonbury's Thelemite community, adherents of the works of Aleister Crowley, run a soup kitchen (whether Crowley is rotating in his grave at the notion of good works being done in his name is unknown). The Pagan Federation runs Project Crossroads, the aim of which is to help London's homeless. It's been suggested at inter-faith events, such as Ammerdown, that Christians and Pagans join together, not to debate doctrinal issues, but to work on practical charitable solutions to social problems that concern all of us.

4. Environmental issues/nature. This really leads on from the previous point about community, but matters relating to the environment (road protests, the proposed badger cull, tree planting) are a rallying point for Pagans, and something of which Christians are becoming increasingly aware: the recent rise of the Forest Church (see chapter 9) shows Christians seeking to participate in nature and open to other earth-based spiritualities such as forms of Paganism. Many Christians seem to be turning back to their religion's early roots in the nature writing of the

Christian saints, and rediscovering the joy taken by faith in the natural world – which is, after all, held to be God's creation.

5. A shared temporality of worship. It is a frequently-made Pagan claim that Christians adopted the monastic and clerical calendar from earlier pagan festivals, taking over worship in order that a newly converted and possibly wavering congregation should not feel too alienated. Although the Pagan wheel of the year and the Christian calendar run in parallel, the issue of appropriation is by no means as clear cut as it might initially appear: All Saints, for instance, has more or less been adopted by modern Pagans as a festival of the dead. We don't know quite what the old festival of Samhain (31st October) involved, but Beltane (May Day) was a time when traditionally the dead were supposed to return. However, both the Pagan and the Christian year are based on a primarily agricultural calendar, with focus on growth and harvest, and it is in this that we may find further common ground.

So we may note that there are a number of emerging commonalities between Christians and Pagans, and perhaps the most pressing of these involves good will. Where there is the will to find common ground, to work together, and to unite in an attempt to solve universal problems, these two paths will inevitably begin to intertwine, at least along their margins. And there is also the matter of healing old wounds. People perceived as practising witchcraft were persecuted by the Church, although to a lesser degree in the UK than on the Continent, and victims in this country were mainly hanged rather than burned. Regarded by modern Pagans as our spiritual and possibly actual ancestors, the fate of these unfortunates has led to significant feelings of resentment against the Church, engendering also fears for the future. The acknowledgement by Christians that these wrongs took place and did harm has gone a long way towards healing that rift, even though it may not be official.

Thus we may draw a number of key points from our evaluation above. Paganism is in general a growing movement: informal, individualistic and diverse, with a strong harkening to the natural world. Its eclecticism, and often its refusal to take itself too seriously, are appealing to a generation raised on media fantasy that rejects hierarchical and dogmatic movements. Christianity is, in turn, demonstrating a greater flexibility in response to social change, and at its fringes seeks to develop stronger, but non-doctrinal links to Paganism, a reaching-out which is significantly, if not universally, accepted and reciprocated. Paganism and Christianity in Britain, formerly mutually exclusive, have some interesting times ahead as we each seek to learn from, and about, one another.

Chapter 5

Celtic connections: Searching for the illusive Golden Age of Pagan-Christian encounter

Simon Howell

A bold naivety

For this chapter, I choose the persona not of a researcher, or a priest – although I am both of those things – but the persona of an inter-faith practitioner and adviser. I do this partly because it was in this role that I helped the Ammerdown Centre stage this Conversation, but primarily I do this because it serves to provide a different perspective – a naïve one. I believe the burgeoning realm of inter-faith dialogue needs some who hold to the naïve belief that simply getting people of historical enmity together will engender moments of transcendence – moments of realisation that we were always meant to journey together. To give you an example of such determined naivety in action, the last time I led a (musical) workshop at Ammerdown, I had the participants of the Three Faiths (Jewish, Christian and Muslim) Summer School standing and singing together Pete Seeger's 'We Shall Overcome'! I believe it was a transcendent moment – in the sense of transcending the realm of our present existence, and getting a glimpse of a more beautiful realm of Shalom beyond. There was, I trust, an integrity in our yearning for a new Golden Age of peace between adherents of three of the great world faiths – and that yearning was enough to enable a shared moment of transcendence where that Golden Age became present, if only for a moment.

As an inter-faith practitioner, when I come to dialogue or shared activism with persons of another faith, I often look, in the first instance, back into history to find a historical Golden Age – an Age where seeds of peace were planted between people of our respective religions. Then I will try to create situations where that story can be told and wondered at, and that Golden Age be yearned for again. I reiterate, I believe that that yearning has an integrity that enables shared moments of transcendence – moments where that Golden Age becomes, temporarily at least, present once again. In Muslim-Christian relations, for example, we can look back to Toledo in Spain in the 11th century when, in the city's recapture, Western Christianity came into contact with Arab learning and culture (particularly scientific study and poetry). The mutual exchange that ensued in 11th century Toledo is well researched and subsequently documented (e.g. Daniel, 1975, pp.80ff), yet not much historical detail is known beyond this exchange. But, of course, our imaginations can conjure all sorts of stories of harmonious co-existence in this beautiful Southern-European setting. My question is this: does it matter if some of the stories that may have passed down from Toledo are not true historically? Does the yearning for peace of the story-teller give the stories a deeper integrity – an integrity that enables shared moments of transcendence where the Golden Age becomes present in the here-and-now in the telling of those stories, even though some of those stories are fiction?

Telling stories of a Celtic Golden Age

That brings me to the stories of a Celtic Golden Age in late Iron Age Britain, when Druids, Pagans and Christians lived together in an atmosphere of friendship and mutual enrichment. This engendered, so the story goes, a scenario where the wisdom of living harmoniously with the sacred ecosystems was a gift from Druids to a Christian theology that potentially undervalued Planet Earth.

Let me focus on such a story from John Michell – the counter-cultural seer who authored, in the late 1960s, *The View Over*

Atlantis, generally considered to be the most influential book in the history of the hippy/underground movement. When I first got to Glastonbury, after being appointed Inter-faith Adviser to the Diocese of Bath and Wells (effectively Somerset), I went into the shop Gothic Image on the High Street, and asked what I should be reading to understand the faith-landscape of the area. I was immediately handed *New Light on the Ancient Mystery of Glastonbury* by John Michell. And as I started to read various examples of his works, I was inspired and eminently hopeful about a Golden Age of harmonious co-existence between Pagans and Christians – and its ecological outworkings – and all located so very close to home in Somerset! Here is some of John Michell's work. Firstly, speaking of those who follow the Grail Quest as those who have before them:

> The first people of Glastonbury, whose perception allowed them to see it as an island of heavenly enchantment. The paradise they inhabited was made for them by nature, but they were responsible for maintaining it as such – and this they did, by keeping harmony with nature's spiritual forces. (Michell, 1997, p.26)

And, secondly, conjuring the legend of Christianity's English origin in Glastonbury:

> The original institution of British Christianity was the Celtic Church... its saints... were heirs to the Druidic tradition... they rejected the formalism of established [Roman] religion and returned to the source of the religious spirit in the wild places of the countryside, for several centuries Christians and pagans lived side by side. (Michell, 2008, pp.12)

What an entrancing story of a Celtic Golden Age to tell again in the here-and-now and, in the telling, to be yearned for again.

However, this story's flimsy attachment to historical reality soon became apparent after history professor Ronald Hutton (a man who evidently cherishes Druidry) kindly gave me some of his time at Bristol University, and, in so doing, opened up his own rigorously-researched writings to me. From his academic pre-historical study, we find that the idea of an Iron Age Celtic race, with a language and a culture spread out across Europe and Britain, has, in the past twenty-five years, been called into question by historians – and found wanting. What we actually find, in the late Iron Age in Europe and Britain, is a 'kaleidoscope' of different linguistic, genetic and ethnic groups brought together in terms of culture. The outcome was not unlike multicultural societies as we understand them today. It was this multiplicity that Greek and Roman observers collectively called 'Celtic'. This culture of people certainly had leading experts in all matters supernatural – called Druids – but that's all we know about them. No writings remain from that period, and not a single artefact (Hutton, 2013, pp.169-176).

Did these 'Celtic' people have a wisdom about living with the natural world? Probably. Virtually all primal/indigenous/root religion was located in the inter-relationship between nature, humans and the divine. Did the indigenous pagan religions and the coming Christianity exist side-by-side in a Golden Age of mutually enriching co-existence? Unfortunately the historical evidence here seems to point in a different direction. Once imperial Roman policy was to accept Christianity as the dominant faith, this was administered in an uncompromising fashion. The requirement was utter rejection of other religious loyalties such that, by 394 C.E., Theodosius the Great was able to order 'the cessation of Pagan rites across the whole Empire'. (Hutton, 2013, pp.275)

Reclaiming the gift of the imagination

So where does this leave the eminently hopeful, and potentially transformative stories of an 'Earth Mystic' such as John Michell? Well, interestingly, a professional pre-historian may well, as Ronald Hutton reveals, not be unduly dismissive. Rather, at least in part, Hutton seems receptive to, and intrigued by, the enchanting mix of scholarship and deep-intuition in the work of a visionary like Michell. Writing in a relatively early publication, Hutton refers to the work of Earth Mystics like John Michell as 'a modern mythology', and says:

> The most precious gift earth mystics have to offer may be that very capacity for fantasy which can be such a liability in the eyes of academic scholars. If prehistory is a time of which we do, in fact, know very little, then the more imaginative reconstructions which we possess the better. (Hutton, 2009, pp.131)

In what sense might imagination be 'a most precious gift in the field of pre-history'? Randy Hoyt, popular blogger in the field of myth, says:

> The decline of mythical thinking throughout much of the industrialised world has resulted in the unfortunate loss of a sense of transcendence and of the value of human life. Some people argue that this has been responsible for much of the devastation of the last one hundred years. (Hoyt, 2009)

The key, I believe, is the link between stories that whole-heartedly seek the wisdom of an older world to redeem the infirmities of the present (such as the human disease that is leading us towards military and ecological destruction) – the key is the link between these stories and transcendence. The New Heaven and the New Earth, or that part of the Otherworld 'where the faeries dance, a land where even the old are fair and the lonely of heart are withered away' (Yeats, 2011, pp.7), where personal and planetary Shalom has overcome – that world is glimpsed when such stories are told and retold. It is a glimpse that is so compelling that our response is to bring the Shalom of 'The Land of Heart's Desire' into our present reality. In contrast to W.B. Yeats' vision in his play of this title, can I suggest, for the sake of a future shared reverential ecology and its accompanying activism, that we dare to imagine a convergence of the faerie and heavenly realms in our glimpses of the spiritual homeland? For this homeland is the Eden that we conjure and anticipate in our stories of the indigenous, earth-centred, wisdom of our shared Celtic ancestors.

In the Judeo-Christian Bible the Prophet Isaiah speaks to a people in exile, a people who had lost all hope that they would ever return home. Isaiah poetically retells the great stories of their tradition – the stories of Abraham, Sarah, Noah and David – he recasts the stories such that, by the end, everyone believes they are going home. And this he achieves even though their circumstances of captivity remain completely unchanged. Probably the greatest living commentator of the Old Testament, Walter Brueggemann, puts it like this:

> [Isaiah's] imagination [allows] a fresh liberated return to the memory, he reads the tradition for his own moment... [he] reads it as a new gift. He does not regard the past as a closed record, but as a force that still keeps offering its gifts. (Brueggemann, 1986, pp.102)

As Isaiah does this, the New World, imaginably the Land of Youth (Tír na nóg), is glimpsed – a glimpse that is so compelling that this other realm, that is just beyond our horizons, is brought into the present.

The shared Celtic notion of 'a Veil Thin as Gossamer' (MacLeod, 1985, pp.60)

In my inter-faith work I have come to observe that we find

something akin to a 'veil' theology in many of the great faith traditions. This is the idea that the Heavenly Realm, that I am suggesting can be analogous to Yeats' Faerie Realm in the Otherworld, is 'a realm layered like a transparency on the world of the living, but invisible [veiled] to our physical sight' (McGowan , 2010). But, at sacred times and places, the veil between this world and this Otherworld becomes so thin that it is almost not there at all. So, for example, in the New Testament of the Bible we read that 'when anyone turns to the Lord, the veil is taken away' (2 Corinthians 3:16). Sura 24:35f in the Qur'an speaks of the veiled reality of God. In the Jain tradition the twenty-four great teachers are known as 'Ford-makers', suggesting they help create a ford or bridge between this world and the Otherworld – thus passing through its veil. Philip Carr-Gomm, Chief of the Order of Bards, Ovates and Druids and author of the following chapter in this book, in his publication *The Druid Way*, speaks of a gateway – a Gateway to the Land of the Sidhe, the Faeries, when, in so entering, we are lifted, through the veil, 'to one dimension more' (Carr-Gomm, 2006, pp.25ff).

'Into the Darkness'

'Into the Darkness' is the title of a chapter of Ronald Hutton's book *The Pagan Religions of the Ancient British Isles* (Hutton 2009). It is the chapter that reflects on Earth Mystics, such as John Michell, who conjure a Celtic Golden Age where Christians and Pagans lived side-by-side in a mutually enriching co-existence – a co-existence that allowed the possibility for reverential ecology to be a gift from Pagan to Christian to enable a profoundly earth-based Christian spirituality.

Can I suggest, in conclusion, that those whose integrity is found in their yearning to reach back 'into the darkness' of pre-history and discover and compose stories of a Celtic Golden Age of harmonious co-existence – are story-writers and story-tellers who, in their writing and telling, conjure a Heavenly or Faerie Realm. This they do often with such a truthfulness to their yearnings that, as they compose and narrate, the veil between this reality and the next becomes so thin as to be almost non-existent. The result being that the Shalom (the profound peace) of the bordering dimension so pervades our reality as to usher in new communities of Pagan-Christian co-existence and mutuality for the sake of the future of the planet we both love.

Chapter 6

Druidry and Christianity: Can these two streams of spiritual tradition inform each other and even perhaps be combined in one path or practice?

Philip Carr-Gomm

There are at least three reasons why the topic addressed in this article will yield no fruit – according to the sceptics. First, syncretism – the combining of traditions – is a bad idea. Second, the theologies of the two paths are too at variance. Christianity, for example, requires the centrality of the figure of Christ, whereas in Druidry he holds little or no significance. Thirdly, Christianity has proved such an oppressive and destructive force, no good will come from Druids going to bed with the Devil. (Or conversely, if you are a Christian, Paganism has been 'diabolical' and modern Pagans refuse the saving grace of Christ, and therefore any attempt at meeting is doomed to failure).

If I believed these arguments, this article would end here, but I don't – and hence this essay, and my motive for attending various 'Christians and Druids/Pagans' conferences over the years: the first held at Prinknash Grange twenty-five years ago in 1989. I do not consider myself a Christian, but then, although this gives the closest definition, I am not sure it's meaningful to call myself a Druid– I don't like labels and find them restrictive. I just feel I am 'a seeker on the Path', and I try to appreciate the beauty and the sacredness of all religions and spiritual ways. I mention this to clarify at the outset that I do not have an agenda of wishing to convert the reader. I know that those who have been hurt by an oppressive, and often fundamentalist, Christianity can be concerned that someone is trying to secretly convert them. No! Instead I am writing this because I think we have moved into an era in which we can choose to follow the spiritual path that is just right for our unique soul. Perhaps each of us requires a different form of nourishment, and we live at a time where we can prepare our own meals – not to pick capriciously at the feast offered by the world's religions, but to nourish ourselves on that which truly satisfies our soul-hunger.

I have met enough people by now who find that a combination of Christian and Druid inspiration feeds their soul to recognize that such a synthesis has validity.

Bruce Stanley has written a book called *Forest Church* (Stanley, 2013 – see chapter 9) where he proposes Christian worship but out in the woods, with many of his ideas suggested by his experience of connecting with Nature and with some echoes of Druidry. One reviewer (among many more positive ones) on Amazon.co.uk is very critical of the book, describing it as a 'mish-mash' of Christianity and the 'Old Religions', which attempts to combine two incompatible traditions, one with a transcendent deity and one in which deity is immanent. Dismissively, the reviewer claims 'if you're a Christian who wants to play at Paganism, or a Pagan who wants to play at Church, then this may be the book for you' ('Davem', 2013). We could get into a discussion about whether or not 'syncretism', defined as 'the combining of different, often seemingly contradictory beliefs, while melding practices of various schools of thought,' (Wikipedia, 2014) is a good idea, or whether indeed what Bruce is proposing is actually syncretistic. We could get into a discussion of whether, as the reviewer claimed, 'Panentheism' is a 'cop-out' in trying to combine the strengths of both 'transcendent' and 'immanent' concepts of the divine, or whether one of its greatest advocates, the theologian and initiator of the Creation Spirituality movement, Matthew Fox, could respond to that criticism effectively. But let's by-pass these arguments and turn to the people themselves who seem satisfied by the 'mish-mash' and the 'cop-out'.

Many people find that they can combine aspects of Christianity and Druidry in coherent ways. People like the novelist Barbara Erskine who wrote:

When I discovered Druidry it was a homecoming into a philosophy which encompassed all that I held dear and it brought me into the western spiritual tradition, something which had been part of my soul without my realising it. My world was animistic. I had always prayed to the one God and all the gods, feeling that that expressed my true beliefs even though I was not comfortable with wholesale paganism. The last thing I expected was for my studies and meditations to illumine and rekindle my struggling Christian faith. Or that they would reconcile my certainties about a supernatural world of nature spirits, ghosts and energies which seemed to be unchristian, into a church which included angels and archangels and all the company of heaven.

Druidry acted as a change of focus; a personal reinterpretation; an altered attitude. It shone a beam of light into a monochrome landscape and reminded me of an ancient church where Celtic saints had called blessings onto rain-soaked hills, where St Kevin allowed a blackbird to nest on his hand, where Brighid was both goddess and saint, a church where Our Lady was also the Star of the Sea, a blessed feminine warmth which a more puritan faith had distanced. Ancient prayers took on deeper meanings for me. Now the Benedicite read like a Celtic hymn.

The druidical circle of seasons was there within the liturgy, sacred geometry was there, though forgotten by most, as were the healing energies of stone and stained glass and the mysticism of ancient words.

Historians and theologians may find the belief untenable,

but I like the idea of long-ago druids segueing neatly with the changing focus of the heavens into a Celtic Christianity. It feels right.

My practice of meditation evolved naturally back into one of regular prayer and though prayer can happen every- and any- where, I set up a small altar of my own again. In its centre I have a beautiful statue made by a friend, of the Blessed Virgin, not a meek, mild obedient role model, but Queen of Heaven, with crown and royal robes. On her knee is the Christ child. At the four corners of the altar I have put symbols of earth air fire and water. There is a Celtic cross there, and flowers. Sometimes I have incense. Sometimes meditation oils. Sometimes this is the centre of my druid rituals. I use it as a place to pray, to meditate and to listen. Unorthodox? Probably. But it makes perfect sense to me. (Erskine, 2005, *cited in* Carr-Gomm 2006, p.7)

Is it not presumptuous of any of us to say that Barbara Erskine has succumbed to 'woolly thinking' or 'theological error'? Bruce Stanley's book has ignited the imaginations of many – it proposes an idea whose time has come, and within the space of a few years has given birth to over a dozen independent, autonomous 'Forest Churches'.

Some books seem to come out of the Collective Unconscious, or from the Spirit of the Times. Perhaps one hardly needs to read the book – the title or core idea is all you need to light the fire. One such book was Clarissa Pinkola Estes' (2008) book *Women Who Run with the Wolves*. Many people never got through that brick of a tome, but the idea caught their imagination: 'Women can be wild and free. I must release my wild woman!' As soon as you say the words 'Forest Church' you get it: it is saying 'Get out of those dark cold buildings – out into the magic of the trees and find your spirituality there!' The term 'Forest Church' conjures up the image of a Christian Druidry, even though that is not the aim of the book itself, which focuses on participation with nature, mainly for those from within the 'Christ tradition', though not excluding other nature-based spiritualities such as Druids. The word Druid comes, according to one etymology, from the roots 'Dru' – an oak – and 'id' – to know or be wise. And so a Druid is an 'oak sage' – a 'forest sage' – someone for whom the forest is their church.

The thought that Christian and Druid practice might be combined is not new. Writing and discussion about this has been going on for more than 250 years. When an interest in Druidism emerged in the Druid Revival period in the 18th century, it was driven by Christian gentlemen, with an Anglican vicar, William Stukeley, being one of the prime movers, and that strange trickster figure Iolo Morganwg being as active in promoting Unitarianism in Wales as he was in promoting Druidism. Fraternal Druidry, initiated in London in 1781, and the Druidry that fostered the Eisteddfod movement, were both promoted by those whose religious affiliations were Christian, not Pagan. Even modern-day Esoteric Druidism, by which I mean Druidry pursued as a spiritual path or magical system, which developed at the beginning of the 20th century, was driven by those who considered themselves Christian. George Watson MacGregor Reid, who was arguably the founder of modern spiritual Druidry, as opposed to its fraternal or cultural varieties, was an enthusiastic promoter of the Universalist Church, which later merged with a branch of the Unitarian Church. This particular strand of Druidry was given a boost to its development in the mid 20th century by Ross Nichols, who was also a Christian, although a questioning socialist Christian, who was ordained as an archdeacon in the Celtic Orthodox Church and performed their Celtic Mass once in the ruins of Glastonbury Abbey. In the collection of his writings *In the Grove of the Druids* (Carr-Gomm, 2002) I've given a selection of his thoughts on Christianity with a commentary. These show that he was very critical towards the church, but felt a mystical connection with the heart of the religion.

Nichols's friend, Gerald Gardner, who promoted and almost certainly invented the religion of Wicca, was also ordained in an obscure church, and the Christian influences on the system he developed are clear. Joanne Pearson's fascinating book *Wicca and the Christian Heritage: Ritual, Sex and Magic* (2007) goes into great detail about the influence of Christianity on the evolution of Wicca and only goes to strengthen any case for the value of syncretism.

Gardner and Nichols were busy developing their complementary approaches at a time when Dion Fortune's work was well known, and her work too was informed by Christianity. The path she laid out wove three strands together: ceremonial magic, nature mysticism and a mystical Christianity. Dion Fortune's work, together with the influence of the Hermetic Order of the Golden Dawn, with its central mythos of Christian Rosenkreuz, enables us to say that modern Wicca and Druidry evolved out of a background and culture of Christianity that was essential to their development.

I've pointed all this out simply to stress the fact that the idea of combining Druidry and Christianity is not new or even unlikely. For most of its modern history it always was combined, and a strictly Pagan form of Druidry has only really been practiced in the modern era from the 1970s onward. The argument that the reviewer of Bruce Stanley's book gives, which is that an approach that combines Druidry, or Paganism, with Christianity would only give 'some degree of fulfillment' is redundant, and reminds me of some critics who state categorically that Druidry cannot be a valid spiritual path. I imagine myself announcing this to the thousands of people whose lives have been profoundly changed for the better, and who espouse Druidry as their path. Flying in the face of the evidence, it would feel like King Canute telling the sea it had no power to come near him.

Neo-Pagan, Animistic and Shamanic Druidry

Isaac Bonewits, the founder of the largest American Druid Group, the ADF, divided the history of Druidry into Paleo-Pagan, Meso-Pagan, and Neo-Pagan phases. The first phase represents original, ancient, pre-Christian Druidry; the Meso-Pagan phase represents the Druidry of the Revival Period that attempted a combination of Christianity and Druidry; the Neo-Pagan phase represents the time of the contemporary 'Druid Renaissance' in which many feel the urge to 'slough off' the artificial and restrictive influences of Christianity on a practice that is essentially Pagan, Animistic and Shamanic.

Isaac presented this idea in the 1970s – over forty years ago now. I believe he thought that Meso-Paganism was an aberration that would gradually die out as scholarship progressed. Instead, what has happened is that Pagan Druidry has grown and flour-ished, but so have other expressions of Druidry, including Christian Druidry. The Meso-Pagan phase of the Druid revival involved a good deal of compromise – of trying to fit round pegs into square holes, of hiding the wildness, the Paganism, inherent in Druidry, which was embarrassing to Christian gentlemen of the 18th and 19th centuries.

The past forty or so years of Druid history, in which it has reconnected with its pre-Christian origins, has meant a refreshing of Druidry at its roots. But now we're seeing something interesting. Movements and ideas evolve through a process of differentiation and integration. Druidry, I believe, needed to differentiate itself from other approaches to the spiritual. It has now done this – it **is** different. It can stand apart from Christianity. And now, perhaps, those who wish to can attempt integration more successfully, because this differenti-ation has occurred. Theirs need not be an apologetic for Druidry, as it often seemed in the writings of Revival Druids, but can instead represent a genuine fusion of inspiration. Fusion cooking doesn't appeal to everyone. So the following observations will probably dismay some and excite others. You decide! Does the list that follows represent a mish-mash or an interesting blend?

I've surveyed the rites of two Forest Churches (remember each is autonomous and independent) and noted the influences of Druidry, Wicca, Paganism or the Western Magical Tradition on their essentially Christian worship.

1. They meet outside in Nature – ideally a forest – standing in a circle, not in rows, as one does in a church.
2. They greet the directions, calling out 'Hail and Welcome!' and 'Hail and Farewell!'
3. They use the terms 'So Mote it be!' from the Western Magical Tradition, or 'Blessed Be!' from Wicca.
4. In the East Midlands Forest Church Creation Eucharist, the leaflet makes use of the Rider-Waite-Smith Tarot image for the Ace of Cups: the dove of the Holy Spirit descending into the Holy Grail.
5. The bread and wine of the Eucharist are paraded around the circle three times, the bread sunwise, the wine moonwise, before being brought into the circle.
6. In the Ancient Arden Forest Church Winter Solstice ceremony there is a Bard, and a circle is cast while all chant: 'We cast our circle in the name of the Sacred Three. We cast our circle in the name of the Peaceful Christ.'

On reading this, some Pagans may feel that Christians are 'stealing' aspects of their tradition, while some Christians might no doubt feel horrified that fellow Christians have started casting circles and calling the directions. But for some people, this is just what they feel they need!

Around us in Sussex we have some lovely churches – built beside old barrows, standing on ancient pre-Christian sites. When I occasionally visit and sit in them in a service, I love looking at the old stone, the stained glass, sensing the history and heritage that this place represents. But when the service begins, I have a strong sense that I am partaking in a historical re-enactment of an activity that was at its most alive centuries ago. And so I can understand the impulse behind Forest Church to break out of that and commune outside amongst the trees.

The great composer and spiritual seeker Sir John Tavener, before he died recently, suggested that all religions have reached a state of maturity and therefore decay, and perhaps that's what's happening. Perhaps much of established Christianity is dying now. Druidry disappeared for a thousand years because it died and it was then reborn with the Druid Revival. It is now radically different from how it used to be. It has a youthfulness, a relevance, as a result. In reality I suspect that the process of dying and being reborn, of shedding skins and growing new ones is constantly occurring. After all there have always been renewal movements in the history of every religion, and initiatives such as Forest Church represent attempts at rebirth.

Druidry and Christianity are two entirely self-contained, self-sufficient approaches and many – indeed the majority – of Christians and Druids will have no interest in combining them. But imagine the *Vesica Piscis,* which brings two self-contained circles together to create a fish-like symbol where they overlap. This is a place of Mystery, of the vulva of the Goddess in some interpretations: a place of fertility and birth. Let's follow that image and see what sort of birth might be suggested.

The fish is a symbol of Christ. But in Druidry it is also symbolic of our goal: the Salmon of Wisdom, the primordial Oldest Creature in the world. We taste three drops of the salmon's liquor to gain wisdom, as told to us in the Irish tale of the Boyhood Deeds of Fionn mac Cumhaill. These are the three drops of *Awen* that come from the cauldron of the Goddess, according to the Welsh Tale of Taliesin, and we are reborn, through the *Vesica Piscis* of Ceridwen. But first we have to be chased as little Gwion Bach and be turned into a grain of wheat.

That grain of wheat turns us into Taliesin, the god-child born of the Goddess – the grain of wheat that stands at the heart of Christianity when it is baked into bread and eaten as the body of God, just as Ceridwen eats the wheat that is Gwion. Taliesin is a Risen One as much as Christ, but for many Druids he will seem more acceptable, more identifiable with, because he is associated solely with creativity – with poetry and song – and carries none of the sacrificial lamb associations that seem so alien to many people now.

A baby is central in much of modern Druidry (Taliesin) and of course so is a baby in Christianity (Jesus). Grace hopefully comes to the Christian, as *Awen* to the Druid. Christians and Druids celebrate the same festival times, yet in different ways, with usually a very different understanding of what they are doing. For Pagans a baby reborn as a poet is quite acceptable and doesn't occupy centre-stage in their world-view or spiritual practice, and in fact some Druids may not even be touched by the Taliesin story. They certainly don't think it really happened – the 'virgin pregnancy' of Ceridwen, and every other detail – whereas, of course, most Christians do believe in the historical reality of their central baby story. And that is what makes it hard for many Pagans, Druids, or simply those of no fixed abode spiritually, to cope with Christianity: the baby grows up to be a figure who is utterly central. If he's not particularly meaningful to you, you can hardly be a Christian. He also becomes the elephant in the room that inhibits any kind of equal synthesis of influence from another path, such as Druidism.

A Druid form of Christianity or a Christian Druidry has to have the central figure of Christ in it, as far as I can see, and so it will surely always be Christianity primarily and Druidry secondarily, and could not be vice versa. Perhaps this explains why I have managed to find a flourishing Christian Druid community in existence, but no Druid community that is also inspired to a degree by Christianity. What if Druidry had something to offer

Christianity in its search for rebirth? What if Christianity had something to offer Druidry: a certain experience, a particular sense of a relationship with the Divine? We could talk about what these mutual gifts might be, about how a relationship, or even a fusion, of these two paths might look in theory – in the future, if anyone ever attempted this project.

We could imagine, for example, a religious community who identified themselves as both Druids and Christians, who had developed a sustainable way of living, generating their own power off the grid, growing their own food, raising bees, drawing water from their own well, burying their dead naturally in woodland, celebrating the Eucharist every day, but also communing with the trees that surround them, the plants they grow, the creatures around them. In reality this is not just wishful thinking about something that might occur in the future – such a community already exists.

In the year before I first met my Druid teacher Ross Nichols, in 1964, he had been ordained as an Archdeacon in a 'Celtic church' in Brittany that had been started by someone who was also a Druid – now known as St Tugdual. This church died with the death of its founder, but it was reborn in 1977 when a small group, who were members of a Druid college, were inspired to start a religious community inspired by the ideals of St Francis. They call it the Celtic Orthodox Church.

I first visited the church, its monastery and retreat house in 2010, and I was struck at once by a strong feeling of sacredness. The monastery is called St Presence because St Tugdual wrote, 'In these woods I feel the very real presence of the Being without name.' And yes – whenever I am there I feel as if I am closer to that 'Being without name'. There is a real Presence there, and it is a mystery to me, and a source of great inspiration.

It is clear how the Celtic Orthodox Church works both with Christianity and an environmentalism inspired by Franciscan ideals and the modern environmental movement. But where is the influence of Druidry? Until recently they have been cautious in declaring their interest. You only really discovered it when talking to them personally, although you could spot hints in the Druid *Awen* symbol by the graveyard, or above one of the saints' icons in the church. They conduct Christian services, not Druid rituals. They read from Christian books, not Druid ones and so on. But in the last year they have begun to mention in their annual eco-conference, held around St Francis Day every October, that they are interested in Druidry. Even so, they are clearly Christians above all, with their Druidry in second-place, or perhaps in the ground of their spiritual world-view.

A friend once took a retreat run by an Emmaus House nun, who told her that in her experience those with the strongest faith were informed by more than one spiritual path, the different paths compared to the warp and weft in weaving cloth. Perhaps we don't need to look for equality of influence in a fusion. Perhaps thinking in terms of a 'marriage' of two traditions, where both parties have equal influence, is unhelpful. Perhaps, as in Jung's Personality typology, in which one function predominates but another companions it as a secondary function, is a more helpful way of viewing these things. It's not about two becoming one, but about two or more streams of inspiration informing us in their own ways – the weft and warp. Maybe we don't need to fuse or blend traditions and can instead follow both at the same time. A path analogy suggests this is impractical, but use an analogy from hydrology and the idea makes sense: to obtain water you must often drill in at least two places. That's certainly what my Druid teacher did: attending services in St Alban's Cathedral when he was at his Naturist resort in Hertfordshire, and performing Druid rites at the festival times.

There is an inspiring Ceile De (see http://www.ceilede.co.uk/) teacher called Fionn Tullach (Fiona Davidson), who combines Christian and Druidic teachings in her work, and whose chants are used by some Forest Church groups and were sung during the Christians and Druids/Pagans Conversation held on Imbolc 2014 at Ammerdown, near Bath. Her song *Treasures of Darkness* begins: 'Since people began, there have been people who would travel, all across this sweet green Earth, in love with mystery, not seeking answers, for truth is a treasure of darkness and the wilder places'. (Davidson, 1998)

I'm going to take her hint and not try to offer answers here. Far more potent I think, for us to hold these resonances, conundrums and connections – to see what inspirations they bring.

Chapter 7

Better together: Transformation through encounter

Tess Ward

In this chapter I want to explore transformation through personal experience in the areas of spirituality and practice. I will show how this affects how we live together even when we are different and how that, in turn, comes back to the personal. In my own story, I inhabit both the Earth and Christian traditions and so for me, as for others, these traditions live better together. The story I am going to tell is one about faith and vocation. However, I have listened to other people talking of losing a loved one, going through divorce, redundancy or ill health and other difficult things that life can throw at us and the groundlessness during times like these are comparable. All the contemplative traditions not only have names for how this transformation occurs, but also describe it as the path itself, the path to peace – how we might all live better together. Buddhism bases all its theory and practice on this process and so it is not surprising that Antony Gormley, who is a practicing Buddhist, said this:

> For me, the real place of transformation has to be internal. We may be able to make very large interventions in the world but they will not have value – or will be reinforcing existing structures of conformity... unless they come from the fragility of personal experience. (Gormley, 2005, p.19)

Very early on in my ordained ministry, which began in 2000, I found myself in the middle of a dark wood. This was a real wood in the village where I was a curate and walked every day surrounded by trees, and it was the wood that Dante talked of, in my inward being, in the middle of my life. I had approached ordination with the idealistic notion of standing in the gap between the institutional Church and the Christian mystical tradition and also the gap between the Church and the culture we live in. They all seemed so far apart and yet I resided in all. Early on, that tension snapped leaving me in a place where I could no longer continue on the same path, but equally, had no signposts to the future. I had to leave the map's edge knowing there would be dragons and, whilst I did not welcome pain, I felt ready to meet them.

It was a time of wilderness. I was familiar with the Desert tradition of Christianity, where in 'the Desert' we meet our shadow, the things we have tried to avoid facing and rather than recoiling, like we normally do, we meet them face on. Jung famously said we do not 'become enlightened by imagining figures of light, but by making the darkness conscious.' (Jung, 1945, p.335) Running away was not an option and I knew deep down that wherever I ran to I would meet myself. One of the Desert Fathers, Abba Moses, said: 'Sit in your cell and your cell will teach you everything.' (quoted in Williams, 2003, p.82) Mystics of all traditions encourage us to stay in that place because it is in the darkness that birth happens.

In practice, that meant shedding some aspects of faith and embracing what just was, in the present moment – it sounds simpler than it was. I started a small job as a chaplain in an arts centre and began to explore my relationship to the earth and to search for others who wanted to express this spiritually. There I met two women who were to become very important in my life and we began, with a couple of others, to celebrate the Celtic festivals. One of the women had had previous experience of doing this and one, like me, was hungry to learn. Neither were Christian. And so though I am now the only original member of that circle, which has grown and developed; I remain the only

Christian, and have now been celebrating the Solstices, Equinoxes and the cross-quarter festivals, eight times a year for nine years.

I clearly remember our first circle – a Winter Solstice. I remember that even though I was doing things I had never done before, like calling the directions, how completely natural it felt. For our circle, we call the Celtic directions, which means welcoming the elements of air in the east, fire in the south, water in the west, earth in the north and Spirit at centre and all around. This ritual felt the strangest part, but I was curious and open so I welcomed it. It felt natural to be outside because, like most people, the Spirit feels closest outside. It felt wonderful and a great relief to be celebrating earthiness, bodies, femaleness. It felt very easy for me after years of Church life to be sharing my inner journey in a circle. There was also delicious food – an organic lamb stew. I remember that evening so well – the thick blackness of the night, the tiny white stars and the warmth and crackle of the fire. At one and the same time, it felt new and like a returning home. Carol Christ explains what might have been happening to me:

> Awakening suggests that the self needs only to notice what is already there... the ability... to know is within the self, once the sleeping draft is refused... For women, awakening is not so much a giving up as a gaining of power... a grounding of selfhood... rather than a surrender of self. (Christ, 1980, pp.18-19)

In that wilderness time, what sustained me was not theology, but poetry, silence and nature. In Kenneth White's magnificent and epic poem 'Labrador' (which I recommend reading in its entirety), the poet, in the persona of a 10th century Scandinavian navigator, describes well what that time felt like. He describes an actual place, Labrador in winter, with caribou tracks in the snow, wild geese and the red maple in autumn. He calls it a time of 'white silence' and discovering this 'new land' for the first time. He says:

> ...I was loathe to name it too soon
> simply content to use my senses
> feeling my way
> step by step into the reality
> (White, 2003. pp.520-525)

He describes something calling to him, 'sensual and yet abstract' that was beyond himself and yet more himself than himself. Through living close to this land and trying to learn the language of the silence there, he realizes that all he had 'learned in the churches and the schools were all too heavy for this travelling life'. As he continues to move across the land, all that remains to him is poetry 'as unobtrusive as breathing' like the wind and the maple leaf. White seems to be describing a poetry that almost transcends the place where poetry normally sits: in the veil between our inner experience and the outside world.

White talks in this poem about a crisis of language and that remains extremely potent for me in the Christian tradition. I wrote *The Celtic Wheel of the Year* (Ward, 2007) partly as a response to this. Because of the unknowing that I was travelling through, I understood very deeply, Meister Eckhart's plea – 'I pray God to rid me of God' (quoted in Smith, 1987, p40). I also discovered and embraced the poet William Carlos Williams' equally famous 'no ideas but in things' (quoted in Wickliffe, 2009), which has been the guiding star of my writing ever since. And so from both angles – the nothingness of God and the thinginess of things, or as George Macleod, the founder of the Iona Community said on very many occasions throughout his life, 'matter matters' (quoted in Newell, 2008, p.112), I forged ahead with a new faith where Christianity and Paganism dwelt together within me. Paganism gave flesh to the Word that had been far too wordy and heady and was no longer of use to me in that form. Paganism also gave Wisdom, who in the Judeo-Christian tradition plays beside God while the earth is being created (Proverbs 8:30-31). Wisdom values our experience as a way to the Divine as opposed to accepting tenets of belief handed down by either the Church or from the Bible. Teilhard de Chardin, a priest, a palaeontologist and a prophet said as long ago as the middle of the 20th century 'at the heart of matter is the heart of God' (Teilhard de Chardin, 1978, p.15). It is in life itself that we can discover the Source of life.

It follows from this, that when I write prayers, I need the quest for God to be expressed through our desire for union not the more traditional language of obedience, a discovery of God through letting go and letting be with all that is alive. I could no longer align myself with the more traditional in-out language of the Church where God is set against the world and people are seen as in the fold or outside it.

In her book *She Changes Everything*, Lucy Reid describes a similar journey to my own and calls the place the dark times led her to 'the unitive path': 'the quest is for oneness with God, with life.' (Reid 2005, p101) On the unitive path, spiritual awareness deepens in a more spiral way rather than linear and so the language of paradox replaces the language of dogma. This means the 'and yet' is crucial: we lose God as images fail *and yet* we find a far truer sense of God. God is no thing *and yet*, God is in all things. We shed skins and mourn where we once loved *and yet* we find new life, a larger love. We leave home *and yet* we find home. We die to a false self and yet we, by grace, bear the seeds of a new beginning.

I believe this language of paradox is the essence of Christianity, but it has accrued the overlay of dualism. In the Gospel, it states clearly that Jesus came into the world not to condemn the world, but because God loved the world. Those very verses though (John 3:16-18) have been used to talk about good Jesus coming to redeem a bad world and so have set up a dichotomy. In the Celtic world, Christ is seen as the Salmon giving his life to give birth to new life. It is through self-emptying love and forgiveness that the peace of the world is wrought. So following the Celtic cycles had a naturalness for me because of their movement from light to darkness to light again echoes the journey Christ makes and the journey of life itself. We travel through the emerging of Imbolc, the earth re-awakening at the Spring Equinox, the blossoming and flourishing of Beltane and the Summer Solstice, the harvests of Lammas through to the Autumn Equinox, the withering and dying of Samhain into the darkness of the Winter Solstice and on to the rebirth of Imbolc again. Of course the Christian festivals deliberately overlaid these agrarian festivals, so celebrating at many of those times, was also an old and familiar thing for me to do.

I warmed to darkness and death being welcomed as part of the natural cycle. The mystical aspect of Christianity empha-sises this but you have got to look to find it – it is not to be seen in the shop window of the institution. I now work in a hospice where death is held tenderly and talked about honestly and of course, when we are brave enough to do that, it is life-affirming. A belief that I hold and work from this experience, is the notion of the Divine embrace where all is held. I appreciate that in certain traditions of Paganism and Druidry that is not the case and a multiple of deities would be honoured or Spirit manifest in many different forms, and certainly there is no one idea about the Divine. In the circle where I celebrate the wheel of the year though, there is a sense that the oneness of all things is recognised.

In retrospect I realise that there were particular things about mainstream inherited Christianity that I had never adhered to and had now shed completely:

1. Christ is not the only way to God. There are many paths up the mountain.
2. I have always believed in original blessing and not original sin. There is such goodness in people – both ordinary and breathtaking. Sometimes that gets twisted and we mess up – in both ordinary ways and breathtakingly badly.
3. I do not believe in the division of heaven from earth or divine from matter which has many serious implications. This division has lead to the belief that the earth is expendable because we are only passing through on our way to heaven and that our bodies are bad and to be subjugated.
4. I do not believe in the divine order of the chain of command that has soulless passive Earth at the bottom, then animals, children, women, then men and finally God at the top.

The shedding of these beliefs is out of step with some forms of current Christianity, but in the larger context, is in tune with changes in the way we see things in the West in the new millennium. Catherine Keller expressed it: 'We need no new heaven and earth. We have this Earth, this sky, this water to renew.' (Keller 1990, p.263)

In *Gaia and God* Rosemary Radford Ruether says that ecofeminism is for earth healing, whereby the broken relationships between men and women, races, nations and classes, between the earth and humanity, may be made whole again.

'Such a healing is possible only through recognition and transformation of the way in which Western culture, enshrined in part in Christianity, has justified such domination.' (Radford Ruether, 1992, p.1)

It is from a place of domination that Christianity has often set itself against Paganism. I wrote the following Lament to be spoken by Christians and before our Pagan brothers and sisters:

Lament

O Divine One, Source of all,
who gives birth to diversity beyond our imagining.
We have failed to see your embodied presence
shining at the heart of all things
and so divided matter from spirit.
We have divided ourselves from your other creatures.
We have divided ourselves from the care of the earth.
We have divided men from women,
race from race
group from group.
We have divided creation from itself and so can never become
    whole.
We are sorry and lament the pain we have caused in your
    name.
Mend our brokenness with your loving kindness
so we may open our hearts and hands to work with each other
for the healing and peace of all the earth.

I have so far described transformation as a shedding of old things, but in the letting go, greater new things were gained. It is now my belief that groundlessness is the reality for all of us, but then, I was facing that for the first time. If we look without illusion, there is nothing certain. In the Christian tradition, we call this 'the dark night' where we lose the comfort of our illusions about God. All I had was the present moment and what was within and around me. Because I was acutely aware of my own vulnerability, my opened heart began to appreciate our shared frailty and the reality and value of loving-kindness. Naomi Shihab Nye has written so well about this in her poem 'Kindness'. She says starkly that before you know what kindness really is you must lose things. Everything we count and carefully save must go. She says that we cannot really know kindness as the deepest thing inside until we have woken up with that sorrow. Once we have done that, the only thing that makes any sense is kindness and it will never leave us. In fact this crucial and world-changing quality is what gets us out of bed and sends us out into the day, to do the smallest, most ordinary things, like going to the post and buying bread.

Kindness

Before you know what kindness really is
you must lose things,
feel the future dissolve in a moment
like salt in a weakened broth.
What you held in your hand,
what you counted and carefully saved,
all this must go so you know
how desolate the landscape can be
between the regions of kindness.
How you ride and ride
thinking the bus will never stop,
the passengers eating maize and chicken
will stare out the window forever.
Before you learn the tender gravity of kindness,
you must travel where the Indian in a white poncho
lies dead by the side of the road.
You must see how this could be you,
how he too was someone
who journeyed through the night with plans
and the simple breath that kept him alive.
Before you know kindness as the deepest thing inside,
you must know sorrow as the other deepest thing.
You must wake up with sorrow.
You must speak to it till your voice

catches the thread of all sorrows
and you see the size of the cloth.
Then it is only kindness that makes sense anymore,
only kindness that ties your shoes
and sends you out into the day to mail letters and purchase
    bread,
only kindness that raises its head
from the crowd of the world to say
it is I you have been looking for,
and then goes with you everywhere
like a shadow or a friend.
(2008, pp.25-26)
(Quoted in full by kind permission of the author and
copyright holder, Naomi Shihab Nye, 2014)

This personal crisis which I experienced mirrors the crisis for
Christianity as a whole. Meltdown may not be the worst thing
that has happened to it – indeed it may be what needs to happen
and what the cross is all about – that something must be lost in
order to gain the loving-kindness that is at the heart of the faith.
Christianity is also in crisis because in the secular and industri-
alized West, spirituality is very low down on the list of priorities
in public discourse. The environment is too. None of the three
major political parties in Britain talked about it in the run-up to
the last General Election. This may be one reason for the Pagan
revival at this time because these parts of our shared lives cannot
be suppressed. So ironically, in the wider context, both Pagans
and Christians can share an awareness of the need to put
spiritual and environmental issues on the agenda and have much
to offer into that context.

For Pagans and Christians, and any other group, to work
together for the transformation of the spiritual and environmental issues that are facing us we do not need to modify our
own values. Matthew Fox says in inter-faith work, 'the result will

not be to abandon one's own tradition but to demand more of it.' (Fox, 1988, p.236) Paradoxically, if we have confidence in the depths of our tradition we can be more generous. Otherwise we relate to each other superficially and through fear. We are closed when we cling tightly to our certainty with anxiety instead of coming to the table with open hands. If we can talk to each other from the depths of our different traditions especially about the environmental crisis, we can work together for something that is bigger than us, which we all share. In this way, the wisdom to be found in the universe can be set free by all religions and spiritual paths. That task cannot belong to one doorway. By definition, it is only together that we can make true peace.

When I plumb the depths of my tradition it is, at bottom, very simple: that we are all held in the loving-kindness of the Divine embrace. There is nothing outside of that, no part of creation, no person, no part of ourselves that cannot be shown compassion. We are not always very good at offering compassion either to ourselves or to others and so Christ opens wide his arms to us so that we might receive the grace of this loving-kindness and learn a more peaceful way. In *Christ of the Celts*, John Philip Newell, takes this idea further and says that creation is good and constantly evolving. There is this central paradox that in creation is union from unimaginable diversity because it sprung forth from, he says quoting Julian of Norwich, 'the Womb of the Eternal' (Newell, 2008, p.85). Christ speaks to us about this forgotten goodness when all was one. He talks about Christ as the hymn at the heart of creation, sung in an 'infinity of voices'. He calls him 'the song of Presence... the hymn of Self-Giving love that sets us free to be part of the healing of the Universe.' (Newell, 2008, p.118)

Whichever way we find our way home, whichever religion or spiritual path or none defined, our planet depends upon us finding the compassionate heart that unites us and living from a place of compassion. It cannot be just about self–fulfilment. The spiralling movement of transformation must move outwards to love beyond itself for healing to be possible. This takes us back to the personal, which is where we began.

Pema Chodron, who is a Tibetan Buddhist nun, is one of the best regarded teachers of spirituality in our age, teaching the practice of mindfulness and meditation. Many of her books talk about the transformation that occurs when we lean into our pain, rather than our instinctive pull away from it, and how, in the opening of our hearts which this necessitates, we can become more compassionate. She talks about what can happen when we do not need to be either right or wrong or make others right or wrong. Rather than hanging on to our version, she asks that we try to keep our hearts and minds open because when we need to be right, we do it out of a need for secure ground.

> Could our minds and our hearts be big enough just to hang out in that space where we're not entirely certain about who's right and who's wrong because things are a lot more slippery and playful than that? (Chodron, 1997, p.83)

Without this agenda, we may be able to walk into a room and see, hear and feel another person as they really are. She says this place is a kind, tender 'shaky kind of place', but it is a place where we can live as we learn to have compassion for ourselves and the circle of compassion becomes wider as it ripples outwards for others.

This is what Jesus, who was a master of the slippery and the playful, meant when he said 'love your neighbour as yourself' (Mark 12:31). It is in the arena of practice, not doctrine, that Pagans and Christians can be better together. For a few of us, that might be celebrating the wheel of the year together, but more significantly, it will be working together for the environment, which might be more political and activist. It might also be offering spiritual practice such as prayer or meditation or mindfulness or honouring the earth. It is in the goal beyond ourselves, not in promoting ourselves, that we can find peace and share it with others. Another Buddhist, Thich Nhat Hanh, says that the miracle is not to walk on water, but on the green earth in the present moment.

> Peace is all around us – in the world and in nature – and within us – in our bodies and our spirits. Once we learn to touch this peace, we will be healed and transformed. It is not a matter of faith; it is a matter of practice. (Thich Nhat Hanh, 1995, pp.23-24)

Prayer

Source of all love, the oneness of all things,
You are the silence at the heart of all that is.
You are in the stillness when the rains have gone.
You are the ebb and flow of calm waters you are the crashing waves of storm
You are the long dark night and you are the first light of dawn.
You are the mystery at our beginning before a breath is drawn
You are the quiet at our endings when all is said and done.
Keep our hearts open to the space between us, the earth beneath us
your embrace around us,
where new ways can grow from old wounds
as we let go into your peace
where all is one
and only love remains.
Let it be so.
(Tess Ward, 2014)

Section

C

The role of ritual practice, myth, music and poetry in each tradition and in inter-faith encounter

Chapter 8

'All acts of love and pleasure are my rituals'[1] : Key practices in contemporary Pagan ritual

Viannah Rain

Instinctively we know what Pagan ritual looks like. Embedded in our unconscious and drawn from a thousand films, paintings, novels – the priestess sits upon the high chair amidst swirling incense, witches dance round a fire in the woods, a lone shaman beats a drum on the hillside, druids gather amongst stone circles at sunrise. They go naked, they wear robes, they 'sing, dance, feast, make music and love' all in the names of the Gods, with the voices of the Gods, honouring the land, the spirits and the ancestors.

We may find these actions wild, baffling, seductive, intriguing, they may provoke fear or wonder. They are all evocative and compelling, for as it says in the *Charge of the Goddess*: 'I am the desire in the heart of man and I call to your soul, arise and come unto me.' (Griffyn, 2002, p.41)

In contemporary British Paganism[2] ritual is driven by a desire to bring about an immediate connection and experience of that which we hold sacred. Pagans will seek relationship with the Gods, spirits of place, ancestors, landscape, season, members of the coven, grove or hearth, or perhaps even parts of their own psyche. The word relationship is significant here – relationship is built over time, requires trust and frequently uses ritual to explore, affirm and communicate its development.

I understand ritual to mean 'significant action' – action which we make while bringing a thoughtful and conscious mind to its performance. In a spiritual or religious context we could also consider ritual 'sacred action', any action designed to bring us into relationship with that which we hold sacred. It might also be 'magical action', which is designed to bring about change either in the practitioner or in the environment. Therefore, as 'action', ritual can be understood as 'performative'. [3]

The key areas I want to cover in this chapter, then, are inspiration – that motivating force for Pagan ritual, the intent which makes the actions significant – and the practices that are chosen to represent, communicate and embody those ideas. For inspiration we shall look at nature, myth and symbolism. I have then chosen four main ritual actions to consider which are frequently engaged in by Pagans of various traditions; the circle, the need for participation, dressing up as the Gods, and blessing cakes and ale.

Ultimately evaluating ritual from the outside can often miss the point, for ritual works on those who engage in it, and good ritual can challenge you, inspire you, move you – it should leave you both changed and satisfied.

The cauldron of inspiration

Mythology and nature are the two most common sources of inspiration for the creation of Pagan ritual. Inspiration is described in *The Mabinogion,* (the collection of medieval Welsh manuscripts that record older Welsh mythology) that *awen,* the elixir of inspiration, was brewed in a cauldron by Ceridwen – witch, queen or goddess depending on your personal interpretation[4]. The tale is familiar to many Pagans and is an excellent allegory for sources of ritual – the bubbling magic potion into which we throw different elements and receive back something entirely new, exceptionally potent and intensely illuminating. Contemporary British Pagans frequently reference ancient mythology, particularly though not exclusively that of our native island, to illustrate, explore and examine what it means to be human.

Though they frequently draw on ancient sources it should be noted that a key feature of Pagan festivals is that they do not commemorate past events. Rather, rituals affirm the here and now – lunar rites or the eight seasonal festivals link one to the present moment, to this life, this place, this season and the company who are here with us. Watching the changing seasons we might better know our place upon the earth, and in so doing we develop the connections to all that is.

To discuss Pagan ritual we will need some examples. All the descriptions of ritual that appear here are of my own direct experience, some are large gatherings for 'open ritual' meaning members of the general public can attend and participate, others are of loose groups that meet regularly to celebrate the seasons, and most are the work of a small dedicated magical group, who are bonded together by the commitment to personal and spiritual development through ritual. *The Charge of the Goddess* tells us: 'I am the beauty of the green earth, and the white moon among the stars, I am the mystery of the waters... and I am the Soul of Nature, who giveth life to the universe'. How then do we connect to that Soul of Nature?

The seasons feel out of kilter, raincoats are not usual for Lammas rites. The earth is damp beneath our wellies and the forest smells of wet leaves. The trees draw back revealing the valley, falling away beneath the hillside, the undulating dragon hill, the snaking river and the far off sea. Someone speaks:

'We know that nature has her own cycles that we can never understand O Goddess, but teach us the mystery of the changing seasons. In late spring the grail ran empty and the crops were threatened with drought.

'In early summer the grail overflowed and the crops were threatened with flooding while the sun was veiled behind the clouds.

'We call up the sleeping fire dragon from beneath the far off hill and speak to the Sun God as Arthur, the once and future king,

pleading for his sacrifice to heal the land, to ripen the grain, to stop the crops rotting in the earth.'

The fire flutters into life, and incense smoke lifts our words into the sky.

Relationship with this particular forest, specific trees, with the animals that sometimes join us or with other unseen inhabitants has been cultivated over many seasons. We collect litter as we go, and leave as little behind us as possible – usually only natural offerings, of fruits and flowers and circles of footprints. The lookout point where this ritual was performed has seen several Lammas rites. Loaves shaped as the Horned God have been beheaded here, their grainy remains left for animals to eat. Spiced cider has been drunk and poured upon the earth as a libation for the spirits of place while watching the tractors below trundling harvest stripes into the fields. We have stayed until the dark falls and the distant tractors turn on their headlights to gather the golden grains. Each year is a little different, as the rituals are a dialogue between their creators and the world. One year the bread was heart-shaped rolls, as each participant broke theirs open, red sun-blushed tomatoes were revealed – inspired by discussion on love and sacrifice. Another year a sun wheel was woven of wild honeysuckle and home-grown wheat and rolled down the hill, a conversation between the wild and cultivated lands.

The rite above from 2012 responded to the dismal weather, which was affecting the ripening season – not only for the farmers below, but for the trees in the forest, for the honey bees, for the animals that need autumn berries to prepare for winter. The intent was not so much to 'fix' a problem, but to acknowledge our place in the web of creation experiencing the world.

Lammas is but one of the eight seasonal festivals known collectively as 'the Wheel of the Year'. For a scholarly look at the

Wheel's creation and meaning I refer readers to Ronald Hutton's *Stations of the Sun* (Hutton, 1996). For now I am more interested in why we celebrate them collectively rather than as individual festivals or their evolution. The themes that inform these festivals are drawn from witnessing and working with natural occurrences – the celebration of sunrise on the longest day or witnessing the first snowdrops or blossoming of may thorn. The agricultural references, such as the Lammas grain harvest, can seem incongruous where contemporary British Pagans do not keep livestock or work the land. However, the desire to connect with the earth rhythms expressed in the animal and vegetable domains is an extension of holding nature as sacred, as worthy of our recognition and – as we are part of nature and inseparable from it – necessary to our own lives. When we hold these rhythms significant in our lives we experience the cycles of nature everywhere, in our gardens or window boxes, through regular time in our local park beside a favourite tree. This desire to connect is often both literal and intellectual. We celebrate the vitality of the verdant oak branch in July for itself alone. We may also choose acorns as symbolic in our lives, a lesson in patience and resilience 'from tiny acorns mighty oaks do grow'. Living with the eight festivals and the thirteen moons enables us to participate in nature whenever we suffer the delusion that we are separate from it.

This ritual also referenced Arthurian legend. The idea of dragons within the earth, and of kings whose health is linked to the welfare of the earth, were vehicles that lent themselves to our desire to connect to this season and the weather cycles we were living in. Pagans, having no sacred text, can draw their inspiration from many places. History, poetry, archaeology, folk custom, fairy tale or art, are all popular sources. The Western Mystery Tradition – the sum of the magical, mystical, mythological and folkloric activity that has been practised in the west – offers us a rich cultural history from which we can choose stories that appeal to us.

C.S. Lewis famously said to J.R. Tolkien[5] that 'myths are lies though breathed through silver' (Carpenter, 1978, p.43), implying that we could not find truth within them. However, a number of scholars believe that myths hide abstract truths and truth concepts in them and that the format of myth – the telling of stories – is essential to human understanding. Ancient myth remains relevant to modern humans because they tap into what Robert Graves calls 'the Great Theme' (Graves, 1948, p.20) and Joseph Campbell the 'monomyth' (Campbell, 2008 p.29). They speak to us of the cycles of life and death, the great quest which is growth, rites of passage, consummations, decline and death, and from those rebirth.

The characters and stories found in mythology have an endurance that speaks of a poetic truth – a truth the soul identifies separate from fact, symbolism that appeals directly to the psyche. Symbols are powerful because they can communicate more directly than words, with a complexity and subtlety that words often lack. One carefully chosen symbol can work on the subconscious mind making connections, and provoking revelations previously unknown. In the telling and retelling of myths, we tap into shared cultural symbols and archetypes. Pagans also seek the symbols that belong to the Gods, or to particular places – white chalk on the hillside, the twisted vine of the God Dionysus – which can be used as keys to connect directly to them. The modern Pagan harnesses such symbols, trusting that stories or myths we are drawn to, which resonate with us, should be explored to understand our selves and connect to deity.

Ritual takes those symbols into the realm of action. By performing, we embody the symbols, we incorporate them into our identity.

They work on the seashore – that liminal place where earth, sky and sea meet. The dark ocean breathes and glitters with a thousand stars, mirroring the darksome night above them, where no moon shines. For they have chosen to work with the symbolism of the hidden moon, and the darkening year. They feel cold, lonely, afraid. Together they have smoothed a patch of sand and arranged pebbles into the spirals of a labyrinth, and now they each walk the path of descent to the centre of the spiral, which is the centre of the self, and the world and the universe, to speak with the Horned Lord who holds a lantern waiting.

Pagan ritual practice/technique

If ritual is a significant act motivated by our desire to explore the sacred within and without how then do we choose the action that will bring about this connection? The language of Pagan ritual is that of the body in the landscape. It is one of movement and stillness, of voice and gesture.

The sofas have been pushed back in the postgraduate common room to make space for the rite. The participants are walking a circle led by the masked herald who beats a drum. When the drumming ceases we pause and join hands and voices from around the circle describe the colours of Yule; the white purity of wet snow, the verdant green holly, fir and mistletoe, the gold of the eastern sky where the sun is rising and berries red as blood. When we open our eyes we have been transported to a place between the worlds, no longer quite the common room we were in before. When we open our eyes our minds are focused as one upon the sacred moment we are creating together.

Firstly we learn from the above that Pagan ritual can happen anywhere, a living room or garden, wild hill or stone circle. Where pagans believe the whole earth is sacred the choice of space for ritual rests on practical or emotive factors, happy to work indoors, but unafraid to get muddy, wet or sunburnt out in the world. Frequently the choice of location will be based on a desire to work with a landscape, much like the first ritual I described. Pagans will be drawn to places that 'speak' to the individual, feel magical or we feel are welcoming of our activities, which want to participate with us. Often simply organic locations, they may not look special although some may have specific symbolism such as the seashore, or twisted tree. Pagans are often also drawn to places with a history of ritual action, such as the standing stone or sacred well. As Pagans often seek to honour ancestors – be they close kin or cultural ancestors – working in places with ancient significance, continuing actions (perhaps processing towards a monument, piling stones in a pool, or tying clouties to a tree) are also ways Pagans choose locations and the action they might perform.

If the whole world is sacred then how do we differentiate sacred action from mundane action? Or express that the activity of the living room is no longer the day-to-day survival, but our special and sacred work? For many Pagans it is the act of making the circle that focuses the mind on the sacred. Whether working alone and lying cords upon the floor, or wildly dancing spirals after a conference, Pagans of all types make ritual acknowledging this sacred geometry. If paganism is defined more by praxis than dogma it is the creation of sacred space by forming a circle that marks Pagan practice.

The symbolism of the circle seems eternal. To Pagans it represents the sphere of earth, the spirals of life, death and rebirth, changing seasons, the waxing and waning of the moon, the celestial heavens above us. Placing four cardinal points upon its circumference we create a compass, and ascribe further symbols such as the cycles of the four seasons, or times of day. In marking out the circle in ritual we bring the whole of existence to us, the macrocosm to the microcosm and in so doing create a space where we can explore, reaffirm and celebrate our relationships with all existences.

Use of the circle has entered modern Paganism from Wicca, as a technique from ceremonial magic. Casting a circle is used for making magic, it is a rampart and a protection excluding, containing or focusing energy. Not all Pagans practise magic and so not every ritual requires a circle as a boundary, and yet Pagans continue to work with this symbolism. From this we can understand creation of a circle fulfils another need; that physically marking the time as sacred in the minds of practitioners is important. Where a group come together for devotional activity, marking out a circle serves an additional purpose of designating this moment as sacred. For a group coming together as one for worship requires a harmonising of intent and attitude. Making action as one, such as walking a circle, is a simply but intense method of bringing everyone's minds to focus. The act of standing in a circle teaches a further lesson still, that all who stand together look into each others' faces, and none stand before the others. Even those assuming the most active parts can return to the circumference, therefore before the Gods we are all equal.

Impromptu chanting has broken out across the circle to pass the time. As perhaps four score audience members have remained to participate in the closing ritual, the magnificent drinking horn is slow in makings its way around our uneven circumference, passed from one participant to another. The woman on my right hand turns to me offering the horn and uttering a blessing that though I shall know thirst I shall also have it quenched. I raise the horn and silently affirm my relationship to my own Goddess and I sip the mead – carefully, horns are tricky items – and turning to my companion on my left give her my own benediction, 'blessed be'.

It is a common expectation that everyone in the circle participates to some extent. Perhaps this is because contemporary British Paganism has no single formal clergy. Or perhaps if we consider the whole world as manifest divinity and all its inhabitants as partaking of that divinity, then each participant is viewed as a source for divine connection.

At an open rite such as the one described – a ritual marking the close of a Pagan Federation[6] conference – a simple moment gives room for some personal experience and expression. Here each person receives a blessing and gives one. In speaking their own words they acknowledge the sacred within another and have it reflected in themselves. Participation changes us from spectators to actors, it places the power in our own voices and actions, for our rituals to have an effect on each of us we need to be involved in some way. When we cease to be an audience member – no matter how briefly – we open ourselves up for the symbols to act upon us – something as simple as sharing a drinking vessel removes the idea of community and communion from an intellectual one and makes it an active experience.

We have already talked about why Pagans use mythology and symbols to work on the psyche, the practical application of this – the *how* – is ritualisation of the symbol. Pagans desiring to bring about change in themselves seek to embody the symbol they are working with.

They drape a veil of stars about her shoulders, upon her head is placed a crown of silver, she is belted with coloured cords. Beads of amber, jet, lapis lazuli are wound about her neck, she is adorned as was the Goddess when She went down to the Halls of Death. When she is ready she turns to face the guardian of the portal, who says to her: 'TO ENTER THE UNDERWORLD YOU MUST SURRENDER YOUR BRIGHT CROWN OF SPIRIT FOR THERE IS NO RULER HERE BUT DEATH.'

Mighty Ishtar removes her crown of sovereignty and a light is extinguished. She is allowed to pass the first portal.

'TO ENTER THE UNDERWORLD YOU MUST SURRENDER THE JEWEL UPON YOUR HEART FOR YOU CAN FEEL NO WARMTH FROM YOUR BEATING HEART HERE.'

She removes the necklaces of lapis lazuli, of amber and jet and another light around the circle is extinguished.

At each of the seven gates she must surrender another of the outward signs of her life until she has nothing left and stands alone, in darkness.

And when she speaks, when she speaks, she speaks as the Goddess Ishtar speaks, she speaks with the Voice of the Goddess and the Goddess Ishtar said...

The above description is part of the *Descent of Ishtar*, the story of the Babylonian/Sumerian Goddess Ishtar/Innana, Queen of Heaven and Earth who bravely or impetuously descends to face her sister Erishkegal in the underworld – the halls of death. The ritual here places the young woman in the position of Ishtar who must shed all her worldly possessions and face mortality. By enacting symbols they become real objects rather than merely intellectual concepts and the young woman experiences – in the safety of the circle – facing death and the dissolution of the self in the silence of the underworld. When she returns she will bring with her a new love of life, a changed sense of time, and perhaps some insights into her own soul.

As we see the whole world as being sacred we also consider the body as sacred. For it is only though the body we experience the earth and each other. In Wiccan ritual the central part of any rite is the invocation of deity into a priest or priestess. This is a magical practice that requires some knowledge of technique, training and practise, but the effect is staggering. To clothe oneself as the Gods is to stand before them with your soul revealed, for to enter into you is to act upon you.

Many open rituals utilise the enactment of a myth. Psychodrama – that is play-acting which works on the psyche – can be seen as a rehearsal for life. When we act as the Goddess and our fellows look upon us as Her, we are able to feel our beauty as Hers, we are able to find in our voice Her authority. What happens in circle does not stay in circle. Whilst we might not reveal the secrets of our rituals, the effects of them are very much carried into the outside world. The woman who became the Goddess for an hour stands in her own power and beauty all week, dares to abandon make up, and smiles at strangers. The man who literally takes up the spear of God or Hero in ritual has practised humility and strength, and it lies in wait in his soul ready to rescue himself.

I have not yet attended a Pagan ritual that did not finish with an act called 'cakes and wine' or 'cakes and ale'. The words and gestures vary between traditions from the drinking horns of *Asatru* (a Heathen tradition focused on the Norse gods) to the blade and chalice of Wicca, but the symbolism is universal; we will share food and drink. There is a magical explanation that fasting before ritual enables one to move between the realms more easily and that eating is an act of grounding – situating one firmly in one's physical body on the physical plane in a literal act of earthing at the end. However, I believe there is a deeper and more significant act occurring than simply preparing the body for magic. Eating and drinking are expressions of the body in nature – by eating we are connected to the earth and the waters of life – in whatever liquid form preferred. In a world of fast food and convenience meals most Pagans will make significant effort to ensure that the food to be blessed in ritual feast is homemade and enough for everyone to taste. Whether it is bread or honey cakes we are making, whether the properties of the ingredients are magical or symbolic, the taste of milk and honey on the tongue, the act of breaking crusty bread between the palms, is an affirmation of the senses and the body.

Food is life and water is life. To offer our food and water to someone is to directly honour their life. To share food is a statement of kinship, eating together creates tribal bonds, and honouring guests with feast is a hearty display of welcome. In the west most of us have not experienced real thirst or starvation, but our ancestors certainly did and there were times when one meal was the difference between life and death. The symbolism invoked in the various blessing of health, wealth and happiness over food is simple but profound.

It is common practice to retain a portion of the food and drink, libations are poured upon the ground, bread or cake is scattered. Because Pagans are on the whole diverse this moment may evoke many different ideas. It acknowledges that everything we are, has come from the earth and one day we will return to it. It recognises our relationship to the earth – that we cannot take everything without thought to sustainability. It may be in offering to particular Gods, to the spirits of place or to the ancestors. Sharing our food with those beings reaffirms relationships with them under the currency of hospitality.

Conclusion

As a Pagan I explore and affirm my Pagan beliefs and relationships through ritualised activity – I participate in landscape to enact and celebrate my place within it, I feel the tides of time and space and season, I enter the other world, the summer lands, and honour the spirits of place, deity, and fellow participants all through ritual action. In each of these ritual interactions I can also explore myth and symbolism revealing to myself a deeper understanding of that self, and bring about a greater balance within me.

'All acts of love and pleasure are my rituals': this is an invitation to sensuality and enchantment, a sensuality that is an affirmation of the body as sacred, and enchantment that exists in the natural world. Our senses connect us to the seen and unseen realms and to each other, and in our ritual enactment we acknowledge the sacred world.

Modern British Christians and Pagans already have a shared cultural history by right of being born in the here and now exampled in *The Charge of the Goddess*: 'For mine is the cup of the wine of life which is the Holy Grail of immortality and the

Cauldron of Ceridwen' (Griffyn, 2002, p.41). Were we to explore together the treasures of that cultural history — the myths and the fairy tales, the landscape, and the seasons — it may be that we will reveal symbols that, in the subtly of differing interpretation, can still be shared between us:

> The priestess is veiled with purple and gold and adorned with flowers.
> 'I am the rose of Sharon and the Lily of the Valley,
> 'I am the mare amongst Pharaoh's chariot horses,
> 'The banners above me are love and my bed is the verdant green wood,
> 'The roof of my chamber is tall cedar trees.'

These words above are adapted from *The Song of Songs* in the Bible, and were used in a Beltane rite, their ancient beauty and mystery evoking in speaker and listener the fire of love we associate with May. Come to the feast, and let us share together the honey'd cakes, and dance barefoot upon the grass. Let us discuss and enact the many rituals of love our world offers us.

For continuing a dialogue between Pagans and Christians I feel we might make use of ritual, the dance and the voice that perform our mythologies, and the stories that resonate with us. Were we to unravel and adapt the myriad symbols available to us in our searches for revelation, might we not explore the enchanted world together and find common themes in mythology and poetry and make ritual which speaks to our God(s), the glory of the green earth beneath us, the beauty of the white moon amongst the stars above?

Chapter 9

Forest Church and connecting to nature

Bruce Stanley

One old name for brambles was *Lawyers* because once you were in their clutches you couldn't escape. I feel more willingly captured by nature; it appears to be the home of something many of us have been searching for – awe, enchantment and real magic; it enables an experience of God that resonates and seems most authentic to me. How strange it sometimes seems that I should be walking this journey in the Christ Tradition, but that is only because it differs from the norm, and I don't walk alone.

Christians like me have made friends with those on paths more in tune with the earth[7] for companionship and to learn and share, but there inevitably comes the need to figure out how to make sense of the journey with others from the same tradition. Together we are in the foothills, making the path as we go and finding navigational clues from our friends in other traditions and from the past of our own, but mostly through figuring it out as we go. Some of us are calling this path 'Forest Church'.

Are we making something new or uncovering something lost? In reality it is a combination of both. The visceral participation with nature we've apparently lost as modern people and as a faith hasn't gone anywhere, it waits dormant (or restless) under a veneer of separation made up of thin layers of 'progress'.[8] The new aspects of this path? Well, connection with nature is inherently a creative experience so the path forward can only be new, responding to the realities of a world under unprecedented stress. For a combination of these reasons many people are more than ready to receive the idea of Forest Church and we often hear a 'this is what I've been waiting for' response. At the time of writing, two and a half years since it all started, there are 14 groups in the UK and as many in the planning stages and it has spread to four other countries.

I very rarely use the word 'Christian' when describing myself in the context of Forest Church, preferring descriptors that allow the conversation to continue without the projected baggage. No matter how I describe myself, some people are understandably suspicious as to what my personal hidden agenda might be and I'm happy to share it. My hope is simply that through meaningful nature connection people will find a deeper motivation to care for the earth. Nature connection is multi-faceted and happens through our senses, our imagination, our feelings and intuition, our intellect on through to our souls and spirit. I've learned from many teachers, but my primary guide and inspiration is Christ and the Holy Spirit I experience as woven through creation.

My path

The first steps on the journey for me, when I realised that nature connection had become a spiritual practice, were as a result of foraging. Like many people I had had the occasional, accidental transcendent moment in nature, but it was in search of new flavours and useful plants that new experiences of God were an unexpected part of the harvest. We would arrive home as if from the most uplifting and engaging act of worship knowing more of God's abundance, provision and expanse. We had been *in* the sermon and we had tuned into the song a choir of creation was singing or sometimes lamenting around us – when we touched and tasted a leaf we had touched prayers and tasted ideas only God had had. And like a good life-long learner I would step back and reflect.

As I built on these experiences I began to rebel against my own spiritual disciplines, which were strongly influenced by eastern mindfulness practices (for which I still have the greatest respect). I had had enough of finding meaning in interior stillness and longed to connect with stuff, creation, specific trees or animals or natural phenomena in the land around me. I wanted to find meaning with my eyes open, all my senses engaged, I wanted to learn how to read the book of creation and understand what God had to say through it. But how to do this?

I found what little material existed, either from my own tradition or from others, a little disappointing – the main problem being that it was based on anthropocentric layers of secondary sources developed under the influence of the separations described above and it often got its facts wrong. Or it was just the facts with no hint at how to develop a theology or meaningful cosmology around them. The way ahead for me as I saw it, and still do, is to focus on primary, direct, reflective nature connection – this path has no shortcuts. Foraging for useful plants for food or dye or booze or cordage and, of course, medicine has been for me a great way to get to know nature, its seasons, ecosystems and intricacies. But foraging and satisfying my inquisitive mind and palate is one of my passions so it is easy for me – there are many other ways, many other passions to suit all kinds.

With my own Forest Church work I coax people along with me. I don't feel ready or motivated yet to lead long structured rituals, instead I make the gatherings I facilitate opportunities for participants to connect themselves, to do the hard work; to select their own level of involvement at head, or heart, or soul or imagination or spirit. There can be simple, paper-free liturgy or circle craft to top and tail these exercises (and in fact some participants much prefer the structure of what little 'ritual' I give them to the more experiential elements), but for the most part I want to plug participants in directly with me out of the way.

One example of this was our 2014 Spring Solstice gathering at Ynyslas, a stretch of beach just north of Borth on the coast of Mid Wales. The dramatic winter storms had uncovered the preserved remains on the beach of the Bronze-Age forest that stretched into Cardigan Bay before the sea rose to claim it thousands of years ago. All around were tree stumps and fallen trunks of what some local legends refer to as 'the sunken hundreds'. What an opportunity for connection, so much meaning to be explored. I had been developing for some time a variation on a contemplative devotional reading exercise called *Lectio Divina*.[9] I wanted to devise an equivalent exercise for reading the book of creation I've called *Sensio Divina*.[10] We met in a circle on the beach and used the same simple pattern of words and responses we use at each of our four solar festival gatherings and I gave each participant the simple instructions to begin the exercise. We met together at the end to share insights and responses and proceeded to share food together around a fire.[11]

Forest Church

Nature connection, leading to participation, as a spiritual practice, has become my focus within my own Forest Church work whilst supporting and respecting those who are finding a different focus in theirs. There is work to be done on a number of fronts and I think God has called together a varied team of facilitators to undertake the work. Some of us forage, some of us cook.

Forest Church began with an acknowledgment of the enchantment already present in nature, the natural worship and liturgy already underway and a subsequent, ongoing question about how to connect and participate with this process rather than merely use nature as a backdrop.

What might you encounter if you go down to the woods today with a Forest Church group? It will entirely depend on who's facilitating it, but despite that there should be a few things in common with all of them.

1. It happens outside in nature whether that is forest, beach,

park or urban green space.

2. It attempts to participate with nature, to *be with* rather than *go into*.

3. Events are site specific, if what happens could have happened inside it might be wonderful, but it isn't really Forest Church.

4. It allows time for nature to contribute.

5. It recognises that God is revealed in nature and speaks through nature.

6. It is in the Christ Tradition.

Some events, from some groups, are simple walks with site-specific reflections and meditations or workshops developing a nature related theme. In Mid Wales where I facilitate a Forest Church our workshops are very popular, exploring foraging, art from natural objects or various bush-craft activities. Other groups put on carefully written and facilitated rituals marking the specific season or festival and some of these are deliberately woven to allow both Christians and Pagans to gather and find meaning.

Connecting to nature

Blinking like hazard lights either side of the subject of nature connection are two questions, *how?* and *why? How* (to connect with nature) is practical and it involves finding a variety of methods to suit different people. The answers to *why* (to connect with nature) are both motivations to get connected in the first place and descriptions of possible results and effects from the connection. The question *why* also takes us to the level of values and principles that steer our behaviour and actions.

Before exploring the questions it is important to clarify two aspects relating to the subject of nature. Firstly the word *nature* itself is artfully vague and can mean very different things to different people. If for you it means green spaces, lots of trees and not too much 21st century on display you need to bear in mind that to others it might be patches of green (or blue) glimpsed in an urban jungle or exclusively virgin wilderness (hard to find in western Europe) or even what is visible through the eyepiece of a microscope or telescope.

Slightly harder to explain is the idea that nature isn't a place or a thing, it is a process of complex interrelationships between seen and unseen elements. The mind under the influence of the layers that separate us from nature copes badly with the reality that nature is alive, changing, wild and uncontrolled because the very basis of civilisation and society (as *they* would have it) is based on the notion that nature has to be controlled.[12] Any bit of nature we can get our hands on is kept in suspended animation at the first stages of succession[13] not seen naturally in the UK apart from on the thin chalk soils across the south (and a few other places).

We're connecting to a *process* whether it is jutting rock weathered only on glacial timescales or a river of melt-water (that we proverbially cannot step into a second time). Add to this natural process the notion of *Anima loci* or *Genius loci*[14] (and of course animism) and you have further intricacies to the connection.

How

Connection to nature happens primarily through our senses – all of them. As I've listed previously, our imagination, feelings, intellect, intuition, soul and spirit are also ways to connect, but our senses should provide a foundation. When, during nature connection workshops and retreats, I ask participants how many senses they have, many say five, but I often detect hesitation and doubt about that number. Mainstream researchers, according to Richard Louv, author of *The Nature Principle* (2012) and *Last Child in the Woods* (2010), recognise a minimum of 10 and eco-psychologist Dr Michael J Cohen lists 53 in his book, *Reconnecting With*

Nature (2007). Incidentally in the conservative list you will find senses such as proprioception, balance, sense of direction, sense of blood-sugar level etc and there are other fascinating senses researched in the lab that are harder to pin down, such as the sense of being stared at. In my workshops I attempt to give participants an experience of some of these other senses. The senses are nature's primary language so when we engage and connect primarily through our senses we lay a foundation for further engagement through the other ways listed above.

For me, some of the most interesting sense exercises, games and interventions have their roots in native or indigenous hunting and field-craft traditions. Connection and participation with even the subtle energies of nature were recognised as being important skills to hone. One of my favourite games has participants working in pairs. One is led blindfolded to a tree amongst many via a circuitous route. They spend time with the tree with their dominant sense of sight disabled and are led back to the start and the blindfolds are removed. When it is time to find their tree again they're forced to use a combination of conventional senses and others they prove adept at using. Often participants talk of failing because they're thinking too hard, but once they let go and engage their intuition the way back comes into focus.

Another connection activity that has its roots in hunting and nature awareness is bird language. This isn't about identifying a particular species by its call, it is about learning to interpret what is meant by the calls, particularly those of the resident, territorial perching and ground feeding birds. It is the language many mammal prey (and birds) rely on to extend their awareness far beyond the reach of their own senses. Like the deer, you don't need to identify it is a great tit, but you need to know when its call indicates approaching danger. Beginner bird language listeners get to know first what is called the base-line in a particular environment, the noise (companion calls, juvenile begging, territorial song) that means nothing is wrong. We learn quickly that birds mirror back the energy we are carrying into any natural space. Skilled bird language listeners don't disturb the base-line as much and they pick up on anything out of the ordinary such as the silences or alarm flight patterns and calls and they can even identify the kind of predator a particular alarm indicates. I've been in woods and have seen deer and other wildlife only to be told by locals that they've been walking their dogs there for 20 years and never seen anything. If you're a disturbance to the base-line, moving at an average walking pace, the birds are broadcasting your location and presence to a radius two minutes away. Long enough for everything else to quietly move away.

Away from these field-craft traditions you find other disciplines of sense-based nature connection. One of note is Goethean Observation based on the work of Johann Wolfgang von Goethe. This is a scientific method for landscape reading that takes participants through four stages (exact sense perception, exact sensorial fantasy, seeing in beholding and being one with the object) as they encounter a place, thing or phenomenon. For me I can see a direct link from this technique to the discipline of morphogenic architecture, which seeks to connect and listen to a space to determine how to build in it more harmoniously. Similarly the design and ethical framework of permaculture begins with observation (meaning more than simply looking).

It is easy to see nature connection as a leisure activity or a choice, but in the long story of our evolution (and still deep in our wiring) it was rather more essential than that. It was integral to the story of our food and other essential needs all of which were met by nature through direct, intimate, practical involvement by us. We're no less dependent on nature now, but very few of us are involved in the food story any more, which is a great shame – we're divorced from the most far reaching nature connection of all. For me foraging, permaculture and perennial forest gardening are key disciplines in this context and hugely rewarding.[15]

Why?

Why connect with nature? Why is it beneficial to us and to our society? There are so many exciting answers to the question. I've suggested at the beginning of this chapter that my overarching hope is that nature connection leads to greater care and lighter living. I think that is a very simplistic hope as one doesn't lead to the other automatically – for example we all know of people who take regular long-haul flights for their dose of nature connection – so other interventions can help spell out what is needed. And again my personal recommendation is the Permaculture Design Course,[16] which really should join the dots for most people. And hopefully, in time, we'll see more of an earth care theology impact faith communities that are still ignoring the crisis.

I think if you remember that we've evolved to be nature connected then it is no surprise that lots of things work better when we are, from our general wellbeing to our creativity.[17] There is a growing catalogue of research into the benefits, some of which comes from the university of common sense. Others are more intriguing such as the boost to our immune system for months after a short break in nature or the increases speed of convalescence for people with access to nature. In Japan your doctor can prescribe you *shinrin yoku*, or forest bathing, and studies are quantifying the benefits such as lower stress hormones, lower pulse rate and lower blood pressure.

A widely recognised benefit is that nature connection is an antidote to *directed attention fatigue*. Work begun by environ-mental psychologists Rachel and Stephen Kaplan in the 1970s (see, for example, Kaplan, 1995 and Kaplan & Young, 2002) showed how restorative even a short amount of time in nature was to our tired minds. It is what I was experiencing when I first noticed the benefits of foraging in comparison to stillness meditation.

What would our society look like if we reconnected with nature more widely? It might help if our education and rites of passage were revived and linked more meaningfully with the nature of a specific place. Richard Louv, the investigative journalist and author of *Last Child in the Woods* is spearheading the Children and Nature Network[18] that attempts to reverse some of what has been lost in recent decades as children switch their time from outdoor unstructured play to screens and sofas.

I was late to my faith path having been rather more Pagan up to my 19th birthday. After a few years doing church the normal way I agreed with the sentiment expressed by Scottish-American naturalist John Muir when he famously said, 'I'd rather be in the mountains thinking of God than in Church thinking of the mountains.' But I took my faith and my relationship with Jesus with me. In many ways I am Druid, if I can define my Druidry John Michael Greer's way:

> In the final analysis, Druidry isn't about orders, teachers, and books. It's about each person's experience of living nature, and if the orders and books and teachers get in the way of that, set them aside, go out beneath the open sky, and find the Druidry that works for you. Ultimately, that's what matters. (*Cited on* druidry.org, 2014)

In the maritime climate of the UK and in the rain magnet that is the Cambrian Mountains, I sometimes wonder what I'm doing with Forest Church, but this is the Church I'm proud to call my home to which I enthusiastically invite all-comers – and I've got a good waterproof. In my group, those from the Christ Tradition are far outnumbered by those from other paths, but I hear the regulars passing on their own enthusiastic invitation to what they rightly feel is their Forest Church.

It doesn't matter what my hopes are for the Forest Church movement as a whole, there is no control from the centre other than the few bullet points listed earlier in this chapter, which were compiled by the early adopters. It is this loose model that has allowed it to grow, attracting facilitators uncomfortable with anything more rigidly controlled. If, however, they want accountability it is for them to put that in place. I'm cautious to suggest what I think God might be doing with it, but I, and others involved, feel the current developing speed and catching us onward. I'm excited and I feel privileged to be along for the ride.

Chapter 10

The Avebury Gorsedd: An inter-faith experiment

Greywolf (Philip Shallcrass)

I grew up with a wary, outsider's view of Christianity. My parents were atheists, my father a fully paid-up member of the Communist Party between the wars. My father's mother was Jewish, so the thread of anti-Semitism that mires so much of Christian history further turned him against the faith. As if that weren't enough, one of our ancestors, a devout believer, left everything to the church, reducing surviving family members from wealth to poverty at the stroke of a pen. Prior to this, the Shallcrass family owned large tracts of land in Surrey, the value of which would now be astronomical. These things combined to make my father extremely hostile towards Christianity and, indeed, any manifestation of spirituality, often quoting Marx's aphorism that characterises religion as the opium of the masses. My earliest recollection of interacting with Christian clergy is of hiding behind the sofa with my mother and brother when the local vicar called so that he would think we were out and go away. Naturally the effort to remain quiet would reduce my brother and I to fits of helpless giggles.

In the 1960s hippy era I became aware of the hypocrisy of Christians who revered an image of a long-haired man wearing sandals, but utterly despised me for looking much the same, holding similar pacifist views and believing that the ideal of human behaviour was to love everyone. I saw the similarities between the hippy ideals of peace and love and the recorded words of Jesus, even if many of his followers did not. I even wore a large crucifix for a year or two. I grew up, then, with an affectionate regard for Jesus (assuming he ever existed), and a healthy disdain for all the various churches and most of their members.

Having always found comfort, healing and a deep sense of connectedness through communing with nature, when I discovered Druidry in 1974 through the medieval literature of Britain and Ireland, I was instantly drawn to a spirituality whose stories and poems spoke not of biblical camels and palm trees, but of the trees, rivers, hills and mountains, lakes, birds and animals of my own land. My self-identification as a Pagan Druid did nothing to lessen my dislike of Christianity and Christians.

At that time, there was a widespread public perception that Paganism was another name for Satanism, a perception actively promoted by some Christians and the tabloid press. In historical terms, Satanism is a Christian heresy that has nothing to do with Paganisms, ancient or modern, beyond the borrowing of some Pagan symbolism by Christians who applied it to their image of Satan. Nevertheless, the public perception did much to widen the existing gulf between Christians and Pagans, myself included.

This began to change when I was asked by Tim Sebastion, head of the Secular Order of Druids, to compose a ceremony to be performed by a diverse group of attendees at one of a series of inter-faith conferences he organised during the late 1980s and early 90s. This was to take place in 1993 among the ancient stone circles of Avebury in Wiltshire. Tim asked me because he knew my deep love for the place. Avebury seemed perfect for an inter-faith gathering. The nature of the place, with its vast bank and ditch enclosure containing great circles of widely-spaced sarsen stones, accessed through broad entrances, strongly suggests a welcoming sense of openness. It's easy to envisage pilgrims from far and wide flocking to it for seasonal celebrations in the late Neolithic period and subsequent Bronze Age, probably bringing their children, pets and domestic animals with them. I tried to recreate something of this sense of openness in the ceremony I put together.

Tim told me the event would be attended by members of various Druid groups, other Pagans, Reichian therapists, astronomers, Earth Mysteries folk and at least three Christian ministers. Tim's interest in inter-faith stemmed partly from having attended a Catholic boarding school in Sussex, an experience that had turned him against organised religion, hence naming his group the *Secular* Order of Druids. However, he maintained long-term friendships with several Christian ministers of a more liberal variety than those who had made his school life a living hell.

I composed our ceremony to make as much allowance as possible for members of various faith groups (or none) to engage fully with it and feel part of it. One way was to ask for adherents of four different traditions to perform calls to the cardinal points during the opening of the ceremonial circle, invoking the powers of the four directions each in their own way. We later included suggested texts for some faiths in printed copies of the rite as follows:

East [Christian]: The eye of the great God.
The eye of the God of glory,
The eye of the King of hosts.
The eye of the King of the living,
Pouring upon us
At each time and season,
Pouring upon us gently and generously.
Glory to thee
Thou glorious sun,
Glory to thee, thou sun,
Face of the God of life.
South [Shamanic]: You, O Fire,
Our mother with thirty teeth.
You ride a red mare of three springs,

Your red cloak flying in the wind.
Through your garments run chains of mountains.
In your veins the rivers flow.
Provide for us by day
And protect us by night.
Light the way for those who depart
And lead the others homeward.
O Fire, Great Mother, be with us.

West [Wiccan]: Ye Lords of the Watchtowers of the West, ye Lords of Water, ye Lords of Death and of Initiation; I do summon, stir and call you up, to witness our rites and to guard the Circle.

North [Saxon]: Hail to Woden, wisest of wights,
Howls of wolves and ravens' cries,
Be sig-runes writ on this bright day.
Hail to Freya, fiery love-queen,
Witch-wife, healer, warrior of trance.
Hail to the Gods and Goddesses all,
Hail to the ancient ones,
Spirits most wise.

When the calls to all four quarters have been made, the priest speaks as follows:

Priest: The circle is unbroken,
The ancestors awoken.
May the songs of the Earth
and of her people ring true.
Hail to the spirits of this place;
of root and branch, of tooth and claw,
fur and feather, earth and sea and sky.
Hail and welcome!
All: Hail and welcome!

Incidentally, if the Priest's last speech sounds familiar, that may be due to its use in the closing ceremony of the London 2012 Paralympics, where a version of it was spoken by former army medic, Rory MacKenzie, and broadcast to a global audience estimated at 750 million.[19] The original can be found in *Druidry: A Practical and Inspirational Guide* (Shallcrass ,2000, p.118-120).

During the ceremony, I asked those who wished to be initiated as bards of the Gorsedd of Caer Abiri to step forward into the circle. This was because two members of my own British Druid Order had asked to be initiated as bards and agreed with me that Avebury would be a great place for this. I had not expected that more than half the people in the circle would feel the same. We had more initiates than initiators.

The initiation was short and simple, having been designed as part of a portmanteau rite. It began with an explanation that the name, Caer Abiri, derived from the habit of earlier generations of Druid revivalists of giving such names to places where *gorseddau* (gatherings of bards) were held. The word *caer* means 'castle', originally 'a banked enclosure', and Abiri is a variant of Avebury found on old maps. We then explained that the key to the initiation, and to the bardic arts as pursued within Druidry, is the concept we call *awen*, usually translated as 'inspiration', or 'flowing spirit'. We see it as the spirit of inspiration and creativity, both individual and universal. An early modern text contains the Story of Taliesin, in which a witch-like woman, Ceridwen, referred to elsewhere as the patroness of bards, brews a cauldron of inspiration (*awen*) for her son. British bards of the medieval period often refer to Ceridwen and her cauldron as being the primary source of their inspiration (see below).

The full text of the initiation is as follows:

Priestess: As we are born into the life of the body, so we may be born into the life of the spirit. Initiation into the *Gorseddau* seeded by the British Druid Order offers an opportunity to dedicate to the spirit of place, the community of Bards and kindred of the spirit. It is free and open to all who wish to receive it, welcoming followers of all spiritual traditions within one circle. In offering this initiation, we ask that you make a personal commitment to walk the path of the Bard in beauty and in peace, using what inspiration you may gain to find your own spirit's true path of creative expression, and using your creativity for the benefit of your community and of the Earth.

Priest: I call on those who wish to be initiated into the Gorsedd of Bards of Caer Abiri and to receive the sacred spirit of inspiration and creativity that we call *Awen*, to step forward now to the centre of our circle.

The candidates for initiation gather at the centre of the circle, linking hands to form an outward facing circle of their own. All then repeat the following after the priest and priestess:

All: We assemble here at Alban Elfed of the year 1993. We assemble in the face of the sun; the Eye of Enlightenment. We assemble on the Gorsedd mound of Caer Abiri. We assemble here to constitute ourselves a Gorsedd of Bards of the Isles of Britain.

Priest: In the name of the ancient Order of Bards, and by the authority of those here present, I hereby proclaim this Gorsedd of Caer Abiri; may it be a meeting place of Love, and Truth, and Light. So let it be!

All: So let it be!

Priestess: Let us now invoke the *Awen*, the holy flowing spirit of the bardic tradition, and direct its shining stream of creativity and inspiration towards those gathered in the midst of the circle, that they may receive its glowing gifts of clear sight, wisdom, wonder and strength of spirit. And let those in the centre join the chant, visualising the stream of inspiration flowing into you, and through you, to energise and inspire not only yourselves, but the land of Caer Abiri and all the worlds beyond.

Those in the outer circle link hands. Those who have already received the Awen visualise its stream of inspiration flowing into the circle, directed through them to those gathered in the centre.

All (*chanting long and low: aaaa-oooo-eeee-nnnn*): Awen, Awen, Awen.

Those in the outer circle then speak the following blessing: Wisdom of serpent be thine, Wisdom of raven be thine. Wisdom of valiant eagle. Voice of swan be thine, Voice of honey be thine, Voice of the son of stars. Bounty of sea be thine, Bounty of land be thine, Bounty of the boundless heavens.

Priest: Step forward now, Bards of the Gorsedd of Caer Abiri, and take your place within the circle of initiates.

All then returned to their places in the circle.

The blessing that begins 'Wisdom of serpent be thine' is adapted from that great collection of Scots Gaelic folklore, *Carmina Gadelica* (Carmichael, 1900), a source of inspiration for Christians and Pagans alike. As a result of that first ceremony, we decided to make the Avebury Gorsedd a regular occurrence and within two years it was attracting hundreds to each celebration and had become what Professor Ronald Hutton described as 'the central event of the New Druidry' (2003, p.255-256).

Among the Christians in attendance was Church of Scotland minister, Gordon Strachan. He and two Church of England clergy were the first to say how much they had enjoyed the ceremony. A couple of weeks after the event, I had a letter from Gordon letting me know that he was sitting on the side of a mountain in the Lake District and writing poetry for the first time since he'd left university some decades ago. Clearly the *awen* had the desired effect on him. He later wrote a book called *Jesus the Master Builder*, part of the thesis of which is that Jesus had known, and been influenced by, Druids and Druid teachings.

In its initial phase, the Gorsedd maintained its multi-faith appeal so that those who took part included Druids, Wiccans, Heathens, Shamans, Christians, Native Americans, an Australian Aboriginal, Japanese Shintoists, followers of Bahá'í, Buddhists and many others. To hear each of them speak from the heart of their own faith within a circle of many faiths was always beautiful, moving and inspiring.

Another aspect of the Gorsedd at Avebury, and those the BDO subsequently founded elsewhere, is the inclusion of eisteddfods during which bards have an opportunity to share the fruits of their creativity. These are open to anyone, from hesitant beginners to consummate professionals, so the quality of offerings varies. Often there will be poems, songs or stories relevant to the season. Classical writers tell us that bards were a part of the intellectual caste of ancient Europe that also included Druids. While Druidry was outlawed by pagan Roman Emperors and Druids later supplanted by Christian priests, bardic colleges continued to flourish in parts of the British Isles until the 18th century and even after they closed their doors, the status of bards remained high. Modern Druids therefore view the bardic tradition as a living link with the classical heyday of Druidry.

We draw inspiration from surviving bardic works preserved in medieval manuscripts, chiefly from Ireland and Wales. Many seem to have been compiled in the 12th century in the wake of the Norman invasion of 1066, in the aftermath of which bards seem to have been prompted to look back to Britain's pagan past to forge a renewed sense of national identity. There is evidence to suggest that this may have led to something of a pagan revival amongst bards, one result of which was the elevation of the witch-like figure of Ceridwen to the status of patroness of bards in Britain, and of the goddess Brighid to the same status in Ireland.

In a tale favoured by many modern Druids, Ceridwen brews a cauldron of inspiration (*awen*) for her incredibly ugly son,

Afagddu ('Utter Darkness'), so that people will ignore his looks and seek him out for his wisdom (for one translation of this story from the *Mabinogion*, see Barber, 1999, pp.146-152). Unfortunately the child Gwion Bach, who she entrusts to stir the cauldron while she goes out gathering herbs, accidentally ingests the three drops from the cauldron that contains its virtue. These three drops give him the three talents of poetic inspiration, seership and shape-shifting. Gwion takes on a series of forms in his attempts to escape Ceridwen's anger, finally becoming a grain of wheat on a threshing floor. In this form, he is eaten by Ceridwen, who has taken the form of a black hen. Nine months later, Gwion is reborn from Ceridwen's womb as the inspired bard, Taliesin ('Radiant Brow'), who becomes the Primary Chief Bard of Britain.

In the British Druid Order, we encourage bards to identify with Taliesin as one means of accessing *awen*, the spirit of creativity and inspiration. We are aided in this by those 12th century Pagan revivalists who have left us verses attributed to Taliesin in which great bard identifies himself with multiple aspects of creation in a way that suggests a mystical expansion of consciousness to encompass the universe. Here are a few lines from 'The Battle of the Trees' (*Cad Goddeu*) in my own translation:

I have been in many shapes
Before I took this congenial form;
I have been a sword, narrow in shape;
I believe, since it is apparent,
I have been a tear-drop in the sky,
I have been a glittering star,
I have been a word in a letter,
I have been a book in my origin,
I have been a gleaming ray of light,
A year and a half,
I have been a stable bridge

Over confluences of compassion,
I have been a pathway, I have been an eagle,
I have been a coracle on the brink,
I have been the direction of a staff,
I have been a stack in an open enclosure,
I have been a sword in a yielding cleft,
I have been a shield in open conflict,
I have been a string on a harp,
Shape-shifting nine years,
In water, in foam,
I have been consumed in fire,
I have been passion in a covert.

Through personal connection with *awen* as the source of inspiration and creativity then, we seek to expand consciousness into transpersonal connection with the whole of creation. A primary way in which we get a sense of the strength and clarity of a person's spiritual connections is through the quality of their artistic output. The eisteddfod sections of Gorsedd gatherings provide one forum in which this can be demonstrated.

There is a distinct and unmistakeable frisson that runs through a group of people in the presence of true creativity, or *awen*. One of the most potent displays of it I've ever witnessed was in the unlikely setting of an academic conference. The final speaker was Alastair McIntosh, a Scottish campaigner for land reform. His presentation took the form of a long poem. I have to admit that, on hearing this, my spirits sank. I have been subjected to some very long and truly awful poems over the years. I needn't have worried. Alastair threw a blue tartan shawl around his shoulders and began to prowl the stage like a caged animal. His voice began in a low register, though crystal clear. Within moments of his beginning, the hall fell into a reverential silence in which that proverbial pin dropping would have registered as an earthquake. As his impassioned poem continued, his voice grew not louder, but more commanding, so that every ear in the room was focused solely on it, intent on catching every nuance of meaning, every sensation and emotion. The poem lasted about 45 minutes, and when it reached its conclusion, there was stunned and total silence in the room, followed by an eruption of applause, yells of appreciation and a standing ovation that lasted several minutes. Nearly twenty years later, the memory of it still brings tears to my eyes. This was the true power of the bard on display, a power that demands attention, conveys information, changes hearts and minds, moves the emotions and stirs the soul. It is this power that all of us who work in creative fields seek to emulate, but few achieve, and that only rarely. As said, when it occurs, it is unmistakeable. It has happened a few times during Gorsedd gatherings. It is *awen*.

The very success of the Gorsedd in its early days proved to be its downfall. As so often, human narrow-mindedness came into conflict with expansiveness of spirit. One individual in particular was bitterly jealous of the rapid growth and obvious success of the Gorsedd. He himself had conducted ceremonies at Avebury, never attended by more than a dozen people, and here we were attracting hundreds. He spread his bitterness to others and they began a concerted effort to disrupt ceremonies in any way they could. Among other unedifying sights, this led to an Archdruid trying to prod a speaker out of the sacred circle using his staff, a fist-fight breaking out in the South of the circle (appropriately assigned to the element of fire), and a great deal of loud, drunken heckling.

A member of the Lakota tribe flew over from America to attend one ceremony, called to do so by a vision. Living on the Pine Ridge Reservation, he hadn't much money, but had saved to make the trip. He brought a spirit song he had been given to share with us. He sang beautifully and with great emotion, yet while he did so, several drunks in the circle shouted insults at him. When I spoke to him afterwards, he asked if our ceremonies were always like that. I explained the problem and he said, 'Yeah, you get 'em in all religions. We get 'em at home too.' Despite his understanding, I was mortified.

Problems grew worse when the numbers of drunken hecklers, mostly identifying themselves with one of three Druid groups, began staying on in the pub at Avebury after ceremonies, where they would pick fights with the locals or each other, often resulting in the police being called. Understandably, many of those attending ceremonies for genuinely spiritual reasons simply ceased to come. Numbers dropped off rapidly. Eventually, we abandoned Avebury and began holding ceremonies elsewhere; Stonehenge, Dragon Hill, the Long Man of Wilmington, Seattle and other places.

When we returned a year later after tempers had cooled, the Gorsedd continued as two Gorseddau, a situation maintained to the present day, with one Gorsedd meeting on Saturdays and the original Gorsedd meeting on Sundays. Numbers attending either event usually number around forty, the majority of whom are now Druids or Pagans, though others, usually tourists, join in from time to time.

In spite of the disruption instigated by a few that drove away the many, I still regard the Avebury Gorsedd as a noble, and in many ways successful, experiment. Noble in that its intentions were pure, derived solely from spiritual motives. Successful in that it has survived twenty years and a concerted effort to destroy it, and has inspired many who attended in its early days to establish similar open, public ceremonies elsewhere, both in the UK and overseas, many of which continue to flourish while new ones continue to be created, perhaps benefiting from not being held in the only stone circle in the world with a pub in the middle of it. It also changed lives. People attending in those early days were inspired to ditch existing careers and take up newer and more spiritually satisfying ways of life. Folk bereaved of loved ones found renewed joy, faith and the strength to move on with their lives while continuing to cherish those they had lost. Emma Restall Orr and I, who co-ordinated many of the Avebury ceremonies together from 1995, went on to organise inter-faith gatherings, continuing the work Tim Sebastion had done.

One visitor to the Avebury Gorsedd in its early days was a young trainee vicar named Marcus. Given his first parish, Marcus told me he used to take ways in which we celebrated the turning of the year at Avebury and translate them for use with his parishioners. When my wife, Ellie, was terminally ill with leukaemia, Marcus visited us and spoke with her. Ellie was brought up Christian and retained her Christianity, combining it with Druidry after we became a couple. When Ellie died, Marcus and I created and conducted her funeral rite together. We shared a sweat lodge on a Druid camp.

What, then, are the lessons learned? Well, I learned that there are idiots in all traditions, including my own, and I learned to avoid them. However, I also discovered that there are good people in all faiths, by which I mean those not blinded by dogma or egomania, or poisoned by bigotry, but open-minded with that kind of open-mindedness that comes with genuine spirituality, regardless of the outward form that spirituality takes. I learned too that there is a transcendent sense of joy and wonder in standing in one circle and hearing multiple faiths speaking to each other in their own unique spiritual language, but with mutual understanding and shared purpose.

One piece of liturgy, originating with the Ancient Druid Order in the 1950s and incorporated into the original Gorsedd rite at Avebury, neatly encapsulates this.

All in the circle join hands and repeat three times:
We swear by peace and love to stand,
heart to heart and hand in hand.
Mark, O Spirit(s), and hear us now,
confirming this, our sacred vow.

So may it be!

Note:

For more about Druidry, visit the British Druid Order website at: http://druidry.co.uk/

Chapter 11

Woven together: Can Christians and Pagans engage in shared ritual?

Alison Eve Cudby

The Feast of Imbolc 2014

It was by far the most terrifying ritual I have ever led.

Quietly people entered the room late on the first evening, Druids, Witches, Christians, folk of varying traditions all gathered for a weekend of conversation and friendship. With some trepidation and anxiety we embarked upon a simple ritual. Would everyone be able to gain something from this modest ceremony? Would it offend or exclude? Would it be seen as too Christian by the Pagans, or as too Pagan by the Christians? Or would it, as a result of this fear, be a watered down nonsense with no spirit or efficacy? I felt like I was stepping out over the precipice with no clear confidence in a firm footing beneath me. Can Christians and Pagans actually do ritual together?

We had prepared a circular space in Ammerdown's stone chapel. A low table was laid with drapes, stones, shells, a candle – the standard nomenclature for any Alternative Worship installation. It was carefully aligned to the directions with earth (coal and wood) in the north, fire (the off-centre candle) towards the south, air (feathers) in the east, and a chalice of water in the west, a series of associations familiar to the Pagans present. The inner circle was decorated with shells to represent the surrounding oceans, and the green drapes spreading out in four directions to indicate the circle of the earth within which we met. The season was Imbolc (pron. *Immolk*), the start of spring and the feast of Brìghid (pron. *Bree-id*), a character honoured by both Pagans and Christians as Goddess and Saint, and this provided our focus, with the white of the newly sprung snowdrops symbolising this season of new beginnings.

> May the blessings of Brìghid the Bright
> Rest upon us this day, this night,
> I will kindle the fire as Brìghid, Foster-Mother of Christ would,
> The Foster Mother's holy name be on the hearth,
> Be on our work, be on our households all
> (The hearth flame is lit)
> *Adapted from the Carmina Gadelica* (Carmichael, 1900)[20]

The evocative character of Brìghid or Bridget is interwoven into Christian and Pagan myth-story and separating the legends of the Saint from the Goddess is almost impossible. St Bridget, 'the Mother Saint of Ireland' (Hutton, 1996, p.134), is the keeper of the eternal flame kept burning at Kildare, Ireland, and in Pagan traditions, Brìghid is one of the *Tuatha Dé Danaan*, the Celtic Goddess of Spring, healing, inspiration, and metalworking. The paucity of evidence for an historical person behind the Bridget legends may suggest her stories are survivals of earlier myths about the Goddess. Whilst the complexity of Brìghid/Bridget resists an easy flattening as 'exactly the same' across all traditions, it nonetheless seemed that she might help with this work of crossing boundaries (K & K, 2012, p.24). The other useful link would be the use of Celtic ideas and images as shared pathways of Pagan and Christian expressions of spirituality.

However, with both these hoped-for sites of meeting, we came close to running aground before we had barely pushed off from the quayside. Having started my Christian journey in a Protestant context I am very aware that the Saints do not unite Christians, let alone this potentially even more diverse group. And with regard to the 'Celtic' motif, we face questions of historicity because of the often uncritical adoption by both

Christians and Pagans of 'Celtic Spirituality' (Bradley, 2005). Yet, if we dry docked every endeavour when faced with our limitations we would never get anywhere. We have to make a start.

> *(We touch our foreheads)*
> By Brìghid's Eternal Flame,
> May we find inspiration and courage.
> *(We touch our hearts)*
> By Brìghid's warming hearth,
> May we find comfort and peace
> *(We touch our bellies)*
> By Brìghid's deep well,
> May we find wisdom
> *(We touch our shoulders)*
> By Brìghid's Green Mantle
> May we find healing and protection.
> Amen and blessed be!
> *Adapted from The Brighid Devotional Elemental Cross* (The River Brighid, 2010)

My experience with Brìghid is grounded both in crafting ritual for Forest Church, and in my journey with the Ceilé Dé, the esoteric Christian tradition, which delights in the Hebridean legend of the *Muime Chriosde*, Foster Mother of Christ (Carmichael, 1900, p.165). A young Brìghid is whisked away one Midwinter by the Shining Ones to serve as *ban-chuideachaidh Moire* the aid-woman of Mary as she gives birth to the Light of the World. She is that aspect of Deity that is midwife and Foster-Mother to the light within us.

Hot milk spiced with honey, whisky, and home-baked bannock bread were shared around whilst we sang a Gaelic chant about Brìghid as *Muime Chriosde*. Then, with the following words the ritual ended. I took the remains of the milk and bannock outside to give to the earth, just as we would do at

Ancient Arden (our Forest Church group). The candle, symbol of Brìghid's eternal flame and the hearth-home space we were holding open for the weekend conversation, was to be left burning.

> The shielding of good Brìghid
> Be around us each day
> The shielding of good Brìghid
> Be around us each night.
> The encompassing of the Three of Grace
> Be around us each day, each night
> Each light, each dark.
> Amen and blessed be!
> *Adapted from the Carmina Gadelica* (Carmichael, 1900)

So, did this rite work? One participant, a Christian, although appreciative of the ritual and meditation offered over the weekend, was disappointed these had not been 'shared out' with the Druids/Pagans as everything else had been. Another attendee (a Druid) remarked that the short ceremony 'was well-planned to give those Pagans among us a sense of familiarity'.

As I later reflected on Greywolf's blog (2014), where he suggests that Pagans and Christians observe this season in similar ways, I realised that, although snowdrops may appear on windowsills or side altars, my experience is that we do *not* observe this season in the same ways. The church celebrates the feast of Candlemas, the Presentation of Jesus in the temple 40 days after his birth, and the traditional time to bless the year's supply of candles, but I cannot recall celebrating this festival as anything beyond another normal Sunday. It may be that in a Roman and Anglo-Catholic, or Irish context more is made of Candlemas and St Brighid's Day, but these celebrations would be different from the Imbolc ritual we shared at Ammerdown. Thinking back to that weekend I realise that the gap is not that great between these Pagans and this heterodox sample of Christians, many of whom are well versed in and deeply influenced by Paganism. The boundaries and connections between us are far more complicated than they first appear.

This is not a wholly surprising observation. It is natural for those of us in this in-between place to be involved in these conversations. If we take the image of a river separating the two faith perspectives, then those folk who live on boats, or at the least along the waters' edge, are well placed to facilitate communication. However, on our final morning we sought to locate a motif we could agree upon – a faith smorgasbord, a Venn diagram or Vesica Pisces (the ancient motif of two interlocking circles used for example on the cover of the Chalice Well in Glastonbury), a lens, a toolkit – and here we ran aground. Those of us inhabiting the mandorla, the almond shaped intersecting zone of the two circles of the Vesica Pisces, seemed to forget that this was a tool to locate our connections, rather than a motif for our own personal practice and belief. For those of us located within this middle zone, our task is not to encourage others to adopt a 'blended' approach to spirituality. It is simply to be a bridge, to facilitate dialogue and understanding.

The Venn diagram offers another consideration – we are unlikely to succeed in bringing together those located as far from the intersecting zone as you can get. Indeed, as we read in the criticism levelled at Forest Church, which Phillip Carr-Gomm quoted (see chapter 6), these folk may question that the circles could ever intersect, and would consider any shared spiritual project as a terminally misguided and doomed endeavour. Regardless, I still believe that it's worth getting this ship out of dry dock and seeing if we can't ply these waters for a respectful approach to the question of doing ritual together.

Forest Church

Under the watchful and protective shade of our cedar tree,

Ancient Arden Forest Church[21] has been meeting since Autumn Equinox 2012, when three of us gently entered into a new way of doing ritual – new for us anyway. The idea and 'calling' to take our worship outside began long before. In my song-writing I am often a few steps ahead of myself. Our first album is brimming with the numinosity of the created world, revealing the influence of Creation Spirituality, even if I was too evangelical to own how much of a Panentheist[22] I had become (Eve and the Garden, 1996). As a journaller I have recorded the significant (and insignificant) stuff of the last 30-plus years, and amongst scribblings from my charismatic-evangelical days I find the image of Christ disappearing into the trees, mischievously saying, 'Find me if you can!' Looking back, I feel that that vision was about this moment, following Christ into the Green – where Christ is and has always been.

This is a pilgrimage I share with my husband, Paul. Together we embarked upon a three-month study leave in 2012 travelling around the country visiting holy, ancient places, and meeting with Pagans to learn more about their practices and beliefs. Ancient Arden first met shortly after this adventure. For Paul, Forest Church began when leading a group discussion on the question: 'Where do you feel closest to God?' Only one person out of a dozen said 'inside a church', others said by a river, watching the sea, walking in woodland, etc. This begged the question, why, when we feel closest to God outside, do we go inside our churches to explore the things most important to us? He noted how churches were like stone groves, pillars arching over like branches, and considered the possibility of worshipping in the real groves. This is not simply taking a normal Sunday service outside with rows of chairs, a PA, and business as usual.

Forest Church... begins from a different place. We recognise that we humans are just as much a part of the natural world as the plants and wildlife surrounding us. They then become sisters and brothers... sharing with us in... the divine presence. (Cudby, 2014)

Resources for working with the rhythms of nature come from Druidry, Wicca, and other Paganisms so these were the materials I studied to craft my first rituals, and which inspired me to devise something new out of Christic and Pagan influences. So Ancient Arden gathers in a circle to celebrate the eight seasonal festivals of the wheel of the year as it has emerged with contemporary Paganism (Eve-Cudby, The Sacred Circle: Elements of Ritual, 2014). The core group that facilitates these seasonal rituals, regularly meets at the full moons for private prayer rituals. Whilst I have found crafting the seasonal rites to be a deeply satisfying creative task, its effects go beyond aesthetics. There is not the space to unpack this process, suffice it to say that my approach to liturgy has changed as I have worked with new and difficult energies, particularly in Samhain, the first full ritual I crafted – a powerful learning experience indeed. At the closing ceremony of our weekend conversation I struggled to articulate this journey in my relationship with Brìghid, to reassure our Pagan friends that this had not been entered into lightly. Both these ritual studies and making friends with Pagans from Orkney to Cornwall has been a transformative process. Quite simply, I have changed.[23] We are honoured by our friends from various Pagan traditions who occasionally join us for our rites, and they often call our rituals 'Pagan', even though they know we are Christ centred. Although gently Christic and Trinitarian, the language we employ is open enough that, as one attendee, Valerie, has told us, folk feel able 'to honour the Spirit at the heart of everything without worrying about what is dogmatically correct' (Legg, 2014). Valerie has commented that she feels able to honour her 'Christian upbringing', and she characterises Ancient Arden as 'a Pride gathering for the bi- and polyspiritual', with the only priority being to 'seek out and honour the

Divine' (Legg, 2014). Our intention is not to convince people of our way of seeing things. As Paul suggests, if our model is the inclusive love 'indicative of divine presence', then our welcome must have 'no strings attached' (Cudby, 2014).

Around Summer Solstice 2013, Radio 4 aired a well-balanced article about the Stonehenge Druids, which included references to Forest Church. Unfortunately, it was introduced by the presenter as the Church of England's initiative to 'recruit Pagans'. The storm unleashed by this inflammatory (and therefore media-worthy) comment was fierce and many of us had much explaining to do in our online forums. Forest Church is independent of any denomination, and because it is not a centralised movement, each group operates on its own terms. The focus on ritual at Ancient Arden is not widely shared by other Forest Churches, rather, the central intent is connecting people back to the divine as encountered in nature. The growth of the Forest Church 'network' does not constitute a generation of Christians appropriating contemporary Pagan ritual, but rather, a small, and growing number of Christians responding to 'The Call of the Earth' (Vaughan-Lee, 2013, p.i)

To hear within us the sound of the earth crying[24]

Zen Master, Thich Naht Hanh, laments our indifference to the 'bells of mindfulness' resounding throughout the earth, with the increase of freak weather, floods, the diminishing arctic, the destruction of habitats and the daily extinction of diverse species, de-forestation, desertification, the all-round devastation of our eco-system whilst we continue consuming without a thought of the future (Hanh, 2013, p.26). Listening to this call and attending to the ecological situation is potentially a meeting point between Pagans and Christians, so if we take earth celebration, care and connection as our basis for doing ritual together, to contribute towards re-enchanting the land in this time of ecological crisis, then I think shared ritual is possible. There is no doubt, however, that this will be an uphill climb.[25]

In our travels, we have heard from Pagans who left the church because of criticism and bullying by Christians who had no space for alternative approaches to spirituality, or who interpreted questioning as seeking to undermine faith. Condemnation, judgement, rejection are what many Pagans expect from Christians. There is fall-out for many Pagans in their past relationships with Christians, and the thought of gathering in shared ceremony may be painful (Cudby, 2014). If we are to do ritual together, then honestly acknowledging the pain of the past may be appropriate.

All dialogue is a meeting of 'self' and 'other', and it is only natural to look for similarities, for ways in which the other is like us, and the ways we are like the other. The problem is that our desire for sameness may cause us to occlude differences significant to the other, to not fully listen to each other. Cultivating a deep attentive listening, which hopefully avoids assumptions about what each other is thinking or feeling, might also prove helpful as we create ritual together.

The challenge for Christians is the *Solus Christus*,[26] the belief that only in Christ is salvation, and theologians have long wrestled with this central Christian idea. A famous response is Rahner's 'anonymous Christian', in which the grace of God in Christ is at work in others whether they know it by that name or not. Whilst some Christians may find this helpful, Pagan friends have admitted to feeling disquieted or offended that others might be thinking about them in this way. Pagans are unlikely to believe in the need for salvation, nor are they likely to share Christianity's hunt for absolute, universal truth. The problem with 'universal truths' is that they again risk occluding diversity. Our willingness to honour diversity and difference, then, is another suggested pre-requisite to shared ritual.

In Matthew 25:34-45, the king in Jesus' story declares that any charity shown to the 'least of these of my family' is charity shown to him. *The Gaelic Rune of Hospitality*, echoes this: 'Often goes the Christ in the stranger's guise.' (Rubbra, 1971) This is not a way of thinking about the other that fits them into our theological system, denying their own voice. Rather, it is a call for action, to go out with the expectation of meeting Christ in the self-definition of the other, through the surplus and surprise that comes from relinquishing claims to possessing final truth (D'Costa, 1998, pp.38-40). So how might the above suggestions open out to assist us in crafting ritual together? Theologian Sallie McFague draws softly on contemporary scientific consensus to locate a 'common' creation story. Wary of a single universalising narrative that occludes difference, she instead finds that '[b]oth unity and difference are in the history of the universe radicalised beyond all imagination' (McFague, 1993, p.45). This starts us off with a common and pragmatic unity from which to start, a oneness with our evolutionary partners – every being, leaf and stone, the waters that cycle in rain, ocean and cloud, the air within which we move. 'From mud and stardust we come,' as we say at Ancient Arden (Eve-Cudby, 2014b). Concomitant with that is the baffling array of diversity resulting from cosmic and evolutionary expansion and complexity which our 'middle vision' cannot grasp (McFague, 1993, p.44). This is a *necessary* diversity – life depends upon the balance and interactions that have evolved within the earth community. To re-locate ourselves within this community it is anthropocentrism that we must relinquish – humanity as the pinnacle of creation. However, we may balance our beliefs to take a step nearer to this – humanity as stewards, or as the universe made conscious – the important value-shift is not judging other beings in terms of their usefulness to humanity. Christ in the stranger's guise, here becomes Christ in bird, water, wood and even stone. This is where we need attentive listening to the 'other' of the earth community, 'listening to what every being has to say' (Harvey, 2005, p.184). McFague calls this *attention epistemology*, a way of knowing that follows close attentiveness to another for its own sake. Every entity has an intrinsic value, in and for itself, and wrapped up in this is the idea that we *know* another, human, bird, or river, only as much as we pay them attention (McFague, 1993, pp.49-50).

All this may help us to acknowledge and mourn the damage done by our socio-cultural collectivities, and move towards healing and change, for the whole earth community, so yes, I wager that, if we can at the very least listen deeply and attentively to each other, Pagans and Christians can do ritual together.

The work of ritual

I have used the word 'work' here, to explore the sense of our collective task. *Liturgy,* (Greek – λειτουργία – *leitourgia,* from *leos* (people) and *ergon* (work)), means 'public work' or 'service', but was popularly translated as 'the work of the people' by the earliest Christians to refer to the church's worship (Newman, 1971, p.107; Powell, 1996). Stretched beyond this ecclesiastical application, the 'work of the people' could reflect on our task, both as the sense of the work we have gathered to do, and echoing the public service aspect of the original meaning – crafting ritual together in service to the earth. This may link us to the possibility of purpose, even calling, in finding ourselves involved together in this work. In the light of this I realise there is nothing to worry about with regard to the problematic demographic, the peculiarities of the particular group of Pagans, and heterodox Christians gathered at our first weekend, which I highlighted earlier. No one can be forced into any of this shared activity. John Michael Greer talks about the unique purpose of each Druid mage[27] filling 'a unique niche in the pattern of things', so when it comes to discovering the purpose to which we may feel called, it is an individual matter of discernment (Greer, 2007, p.216). We can perhaps hold the idea of 'calling' to the project, whether that be a sense of our deities urging us to get involved, or whether it is simply something we fancy doing, either way, we follow the tug in the soul which helps us figure out the tasks that are ours to do.

A vast array of activities contend for inclusion in the general category of 'ritual', so it is impossible to attempt a full definition and classification (Grimes, 2014, pp.197 cf.185-210). Besides, as a *ritualist*, to use Grimes' term, my concern here is more pragmatic than analytical – seeking a starting point for re-inventing, re-imagining rites in an inter-religious context (Grimes, 2014, p.192). To help us appreciate how ritual might work for us, or how we might do ritual work together, or how we might ensure our rituals work, I would like to use the idea of ritual as *performance* (Bell, 1997, pp.72-76).

Previous theories have tended to see ritual as a secondary acting-out of tradition, or the 'formal expression of doctrine' (Davies, 2002, p.112 & 115) in which ritual is the offspring of belief or mythic narrative. Performance resists this logocentric approach to some degree. It helps us approach ritual as an *embodied event*, a process in which the many levels of ritual activity – textual, gestural, sensual, motional and emotional – converge in the unfolding of the event (Grimes, 2010, p.92). In ritual *framing*, these different activities trigger associations via shared interpretive frameworks, and an example of this is the preparation of the space for and the use of Celtic-style language in the opening ritual quoted earlier. Framing allows us to ensure that ritual participants from different spiritual traditions may find a touchstone or two within the rites we may craft together, even if one frame may trigger different sets of understandings.

Logocentric approaches assume that the symbolic system expressed in a ritual is coherent. However, as Grimes observes, ritual borrows and appropriates so many different symbols, that to lay them out in a neat pattern would reveal the inconsistencies and contradictions. The nature of performance as an unfolding event negotiates and holds these incoherencies. This is particularly useful for us, as we are hoping to craft ritual together with colleagues from many seemingly conflicting traditions, and my hope is that we would restrain ourselves from forcing coherency on the disparate myths and beliefs that we may be seeking to combine. It is dramaturgy that is the organising principle of ritual as performance, rather than theology. So there is an aesthetic to our collegial ritual crafting. 'Beauty is truth, truth beauty,' said Keats, and questions of beauty are more about personal preferences, as Harvey notes, 'discussions of 'beauty' are rarely deadly', unlike the conflict solicited by the search for 'truth' (Harvey, 1997, p.216). Another useful corollary of this understanding is that those of us involved in the ritual will have different beliefs and philosophies about what is actually going on and ritual helps us to foreground *praxis* over *doxis*.

The decentring of text shines a light on the interrelated questions of *efficacy* and *agency* – how a ritual works on us and how ritual participants can change their worlds. *Efficacy* is the 'work' of the ritual, what it achieves. The problem with this is that ritual and liturgy are often accorded a rarefied status in which a means-end word such as 'work' does not fit – should we be looking to ritual to achieve practical ends? (Grimes, 2014, pp.297-8). In the early days of religious studies, a non-utilitarian quality was used to differentiate 'real worship' from the non-rational 'magic' of primitive acts aimed at practical results such as healing or bringing rain (Bell, 1997, p.46). This distinction has on the whole been abandoned because of the cultural biases it demonstrated. However, it is important for our purposes, because for many contemporary Pagans, magic is a crucial category of practice, and not a pejorative term for the practices of primitives and Catholics (Bell, 1997, p.52).[28]

In the performance theories of the late 20th century, the concept of efficacy has marked a return to prominence of the idea of 'magic', albeit transposed into a cultural key. Effective rites are measured by the transformations or transpositions that are achieved whether cultural, communal or personal, and 'depend on inheriting, discovering, or inventing value-laden images that are driven deeply, by repeated practice and performance, into the marrow' (Grimes, 2000, p.5). Efficacy, then, is measured by the achievement of some manner of transformation, and for us this is the magical work of ritual, or rather the magical working within ritual. Christians working alongside Pagans in crafting ritual will need to come to terms with the word 'magic', and all the different meanings it will have for the participants. Those whose faith has been shaped by Protestant Christianity, may find that 'magic' does not sit comfortably, even though they may be at ease with the idea of the Holy Spirit at work in the world. Christians will therefore need to re-interpret or balance it for themselves in authentic ways that allows respectful appreciation and possibly some level of participation.

Interrelated with the idea of efficacy, is the idea of *agency*. Ritual actors, or agents, are not passive recipients of symbolic meanings, but are active in their creative reinterpretation, re-appropriation and re-creation. Ritual can then be seen as a vehicle for cultural and social change, as participants 'fashion rituals that mold their world'. The concept of *agency* in ritual theory does tend to be purely humanistic, or at the very least the 'beyond' category is social rather than divine. An evocative anthropological model for agency is offered by Apffel-Marglin. Through her study of Andean and Amazonian indigenous ritual reconstruction, she sees ritual as 'regenerating liveable worlds', which refers to the harmonious balance of all the participants within a particular pacha (world). She suggests three levels of agency: human, non-human (animals, plants, water, soil, wind, etc.), and other-than-human (nature spirits, deities, ancestors). Although I suggested that offering a definition of ritual was impossible, I would like to relate Apffel-Marglin's. She understands rituals as:

...actions by which humans, non-humans, and other-than-humans intra-act, and mutually weave each other into an achieved continuity, into an achieved liveable and regenerated world... What separates out ritual action [is that] the patterning of actions is designed to... synchronise the awareness of the different participants – human, non-human, and other-than-human. (Apffel-Marglin, 2011, pp.163-4)[29]

This is very suggestive for the possibilities of ritual. I am convinced that it is gently, quietly transformative, as it has been for me, and much of this is the soft journeying around the year with a different set of understandings and approaches, creating a new world out of the old one. For example, becoming more attentive to the land within which Ancient Arden meets for ritual has led to the unexpected emerging of what some may consider irrational superstition, but which I feel is just a gently deepening sensitivity to the signs and traces of communication from non-humans and other-than-humans. What is required, I suggest, is an open-hearted and open-minded approach to the subjunctive world of ritual, the playful as-if experimenting with a different identity, a different way of being in the world. It can help us shift our thinking away from an anthropocentric worldview, and change how we act in the world – if we let it. This I think approaches the work of ritual that we should be looking at.

Re-enchanted world

'Celebrating Planet Earth' was well chosen as the title of our weekend of conversation reflecting, as it does, the concern on the minds of Pagans and Christians alike with regard to the ecological situation of the planet and the challenge of climate change. I hope I have shown above that it might be possible to do ritual together, and I would go further to suggest that we should be doing ritual together, and this is because I think our primary ritual task is to contribute to the re-enchantment of the world.

Greer traces the disenchantment of the world to the spread

throughout Western Europe of the ideas of scientific materialism, the mechanistic model of the universe and its expression in the Industrial Revolution. He talks about the loss of the flow of enchantment in the world, and this is echoed by Apffel-Marglin, who characterised pre-modern Europe as filled with 'an abundance of beings' who 'taught us to share the bounty of the world... the gestures of reciprocity'. In the wake of the progress of the rationalist Western hegemony, these beings became 'natural resources', without agency (Apffel-Marglin, 2011, pp.3-4). Magic, in Greer's understanding, is the flow or force of life, 'rooted in our connectedness' with the earth, and that magic works to deepen those connections (Greer, 2007, p.ix). I would like to identify two main aspects of the work of re-enchantment through ritual.

First, the aim of re-enchantment is a transformation – a magic – which works on *us*. This task involves changing the way we see things, shifting consciousness to precipitate a more connected way of living, and recognising ourselves as not separate from the web of relationships that connect the earth communities, human, non-human, and other-than-human. Despite the way our rational, mechanistic worldview provides us with the illusion of a privileged position or perspective from outside the web, we are instead fully interwoven within it, such that our actions have consequences for every other being in this network of inter-relations. This is the magic we are seeking to do in ritual. To change *us*. This is a constant ongoing process of driving this new paradigm 'deeply into the bone' (Grimes, 2000). Christians need to get plugged back in to their earth-home and although being a Pagan might provide a head-start, I am sure that most would agree that there is always space to deepen, strengthen, and radicalise our connectedness in the web. And ritual can help. If more of us can achieve these transformations then we can change our worlds by changing how we see them, which changes how we live in them (McFague, 1993, p.91).

The second aspect of re-enchanting the land, is in more focused rituals and ceremonies such as healing and cleansing the land, working with a particular location to regenerate the worlds of reciprocal relations between the various communities there. John Michael Greer has some interesting ideas in his *Druid Magic Handbook,* and whilst the specificity of the ceremonial Druid magical rites that he outlines may not be transferable into our shared context, the practical suggestions he makes are a good starting point. He offers a land-cleansing ritual for the healing and cleansing of a piece of land from the poisons, depletions and damage of modern western industrial society. Such rituals of healing intention and prayer for the land in combination with practical activities such as clearing rubbish and planting trees can effect subtle shifts. We have certainly found a gentle change in our back garden over the time we have been doing Forest Church there. Of particular interest is the caution he voices in choosing the right location. An already well known beauty spot or sacred place is probably not appropriate, and Greer suggests *refugia,* which for ecologists are beleaguered patches of nature on the fringes and boundaries of the industrial world, which are often filled with human refuse, or which spring up in the abandoned sites of human activity, breaking through the concrete. Clearing out rubbish, planting trees and blessing the place with rituals of cleansing, healing and celebration can help to create new sacred spaces in the little corners of our disenchanted world. From such places, the re-enchantment of the world can flow outward, to help us once again to recognise the sacrality of the world, to cleanse the toxins of our avarice and selfishness, and to enter into reciprocal relationships with all the life forms woven into the network of the earth community. This latter aspect of the re-enchantment work of ritual helps to ground our work in its necessary local focus. Although the global context may inspire our thinking and ritualising, is not the meaningful location of that work, instead, our ritual creation must arise from the specificity of place.

So we may choose to do rituals of healing, of fertility, listening and connecting to create new sacred spaces, and perhaps more general ceremonies of thanksgiving and celebration and reciprocity. Whatever we decide to do, my suggestion is that the event should be crafted in two ways, collegially and in workshop. My use of 'collegial' follows McFague's suggestion for an appropriate model for doing theology in the light of the ecological crisis, which starts with an agreement of a broadly common agenda, in our case the celebration of the earth as our home, and the re-enchantment of the world. Implied in collegiality is the recognition that because our agenda is so broad, we need many and diverse voices involved in the work. Diversity should be 'sought out and applauded' not simply shown respect. Our ritual work then, could be a 'crazy patchwork quilt', haphazard and idiosyncratic, but useable nonetheless (McFague, 1993, pp.67-8). The collegial approach is about suggesting alternatives to each other and negotiating differences – honestly and with attentive listening, celebrating our diversity, which is itself only one aspect of the vast diversity of the biotic community.

I'd like to take it further than McFague, however, following on from the question of agency briefly covered above, that this collegiality is extended beyond the human partners of our ritual activity together. And this is where the second consideration, workshop, comes in. Once we have located a place in which we wish to perform a rite of some kind – or find that the place, or the divine, calls us to work ritual there – we need to spend time together in the space, practising what we believe, and consulting the wider biotic community of that place, sitting in council with *all* the life forms there. A workshop then suggests a process, maybe a number of workshops, in which we share together the different ways we have developed in our variations traditions that help us connect to and listen to this wider council. Simply being out together in nature and learning from each other with open-minded willingness to try something new is a good start to our project. From this we can devise our ritual with the collegial voices of all our relatives 'whether they have fins or roots' (LaDuke, 2013, p.87).

With the urgent need to effect some kind of shift in how we live in the world from one of oblivious consumption to one of reciprocal partnership, and to remember that 'together we are woven into the web of being' (Eve-Cudby, 2014b), I think that not only can we do ritual together, but that we must, trusting in the council of Spirit, animals, plants, soil and rock, in the birds, and in each other.

I will smoor the fire as Brìghid, Foster-Mother of Christ would,
The blessings of Brìghid the Bright be on the hearth,
Be on our work, be on our households all
(*The hearth flame is extinguished*).

Conclusion and reflections

Chapter 12

Where next?: Suggestions for practical ways of going forward

Denise Cush

Many participants in the Conversation considered that the experience had been very positive, and that something new had started. There follows an analysis of the weaknesses and strengths of the event, drawing upon evaluations from participants, our hosts at Ammerdown and my own reflections.

We perhaps spent too much time on clearing away the debris of past misunderstanding, rather than looking at the positive contributions that each tradition made to the lives of its adherents, which did not come across as strongly. This is somewhat remedied by the chapters in this book, especially in Section C. These chapters were contributed by participants who were not speakers at the event, and chosen to highlight the value of ritual, story and creativity in each tradition and across traditions.

There was insufficient time to really develop the role of ecological awareness and environmental activism as an arena for co-operation between Pagans and Christians, as had been hoped from the original title 'Celebrating Planet Earth'. We did, however, engage in some shared ritual celebration of the earth in the course of the weekend. Paganism is more obviously rooted in nature, as we can see from the definition offered by the Pagan Federation 'a polytheistic or pantheistic nature-worshipping religion' (2014). It might be argued, however, that the highlighting of the ecological agenda by contemporary Pagans is in part because it is a relatively new tradition, which grew up the era where we have become more aware of the threats to our planet. In literature on religion and ecology (such as World Wide Fund for Nature/Cassell's series *World Religions and Ecology*), there is a tendency for every religious tradition except Christianity to argue that it has been environmental for millennia, whereas contributions from Christianity (e.g. Breuilly and Palmer, 1992) are full of apologies and promises to do better in the future (Christianity being a religion of repentance and forgiveness, and having been blamed for our environmental ills in influential sources such as White, 1997). Such self-images on the part of religious traditions are somewhat anachronistic and one-sided, and there are both environmentally positive and negative teachings and impacts to be found in most traditions. Christianity as well as Paganism has environmentally aware strands, as exemplified by Matthew Fox (e.g. 1991), the Forest Church movement (see chapter 9), and the revival of 'natural theology' (see for example McGrath, 2008).

Nevertheless, at this particular gathering, perhaps our sample of Christians was rather unrepresentative, in that they were chosen for an interest in nature and openness to other nature-based spiritualities. This is an issue for many inter-faith dialogue exercises, in that mostly the more 'liberal' wing of any tradition gets involved. Another imbalance was the whereas the represen-tatives of Paganism included people such as the leaders of the Order of Bards, Ovates and Druids, and of the British Druid Order ('Pagan royalty' in the words of one participant) we did not have the Archbishop of Canterbury, or Cardinal Vincent Nichols. This probably says more about the current relative sizes of the traditions in this country than anything else.

Graham Harvey reminded us of the real differences between the teachings of Christianity and Paganism, and some disap-pointment was expressed that we did not really get into theological debate. There is only so much that can be covered in a weekend, and perhaps relationships were more important than theology at this stage. Ideas about the divine, salvation, enchantment, life after death, really do differ, and there is no point in pretending everyone thinks the same 'really'. As Graham writes, quoting William Blake, 'opposition is true friendship', or in the words of Tagore, 'The problem is not how to wipe out all differences, but how to unite with all differences intact.' (1961, p.146) One difficulty is that Christian theology has a long history and bibliography, whereas Pagan theology is still under construction (but see for example, York, 2003). There are already people such as Paul Cudby working on theologies that attempt to reconcile animism and theism, and interesting things could develop.

In the expression of theology, Pagans are perhaps more explicit than Christians that the language used to express beliefs and values is that of story, myth and symbol, creatively used, rather than that of philosophical propositions or revealed doctrines. Some Christians, such as those belonging to the Sea of Faith network,[30] are comfortable with seeing religion as a human creation, but the majority would find that a step too far.

One way of uniting people is to find a common enemy, and I observed examples beginning to emerge during the Conversation. Candidates included 'secularists', 'Protestants', 'fundamentalists', and 'scientists' (or perhaps 'sciencists'). We did notice what was happening though and stopped.

Turning to the strengths and achievements of the Conversation, like Simon Howell, I have a strong (if perhaps, as he says, 'naïve') belief that simply meeting, talking to and eating with 'the other' has great benefits (see chapter 5). I might not use the language of 'moments of transcendence' to describe what can happen, but I certainly know from many years of organising student placements in religious communities not their own,[31] or even just taking them on a visit to a place of worship, that simply encountering the 'other' as a real person can be life-changing.

We can discover some concepts and actions shared by (many) Pagans and (many) Christians. The very acknowledgement that there is a spiritual dimension to human experience, however this is expressed, is a start. In spite of some stereotypes, both traditions base their ethics on love and compassion to others. Augustine's 'love and do what thou wilt' is not so different from the 'an' it harm none, do what thou wilt' of the Wiccan Rede. Paganism more obviously stresses the immanence of the divine in nature, yet central teachings of Christianity such as the Incarnation and the Holy Spirit, also require the divine to be immanent in the material world, an aspect stressed in Orthodox spirituality. Both traditions on the whole find great value in ritual and ceremony, story and music to express the ineffable and to actually bring about transformation.

Most Christians, at least in the past few decades, have realised the pressing need to address environmental concerns, and can join with Pagans in this endeavour, as was emphasised by the original title of the Conversation. Both traditions exhibit a tension between spirituality as a form of individual personal development and the understanding that we are in a web of relationships with human community and with the other-than-human world. Pagans and Christians can join in practical action together in spite of theological differences. I recall when visiting the Greenham Common peace camp in the 1980s, there were Quakers, Catholics and Pagans, all able to join in singing, 'You can't kill the spirit, she goes on and on.'

Many of the festival times celebrated by Pagans and Christians coincide – our Conversation took place during Imbolc/Candlemas. Although would seem natural to assume that Christianity borrowed aspects of ancient pagan festivals as part of a process of indigenisation (an assumption fuelled by 19th and 20th century armchair anthropologists and folklorists), historians such as Ronald Hutton (1991, 1999) tell us that it is much more complicated, some festivals are more recent than we think, and there have probably been influences in both directions, as well as some mere co-incidence. Although the Pagan festivals of

Samhain, Imbolc, Beltane and Lughnasa are attested by medieval sources to be ancient Irish (and in part more widely Celtic) festivals, and some Christmas, May and midsummer customs 'descended directly from pagan rituals' (Hutton, 1999, p.122) the combination with the solstices and equinoxes into the contemporary Pagan eight festival wheel seems to have been of recent origin. Ronald Hutton tells us that it was a product of the early development of Wicca in the 1950s, being approved by Gerald Gardner in 1958 and adopted by Ross Nichols for Druidry in 1964 (Hutton, 1999, p.248). In any case, it is also natural for people of any tradition and none to light fires and lamps to mark the nights drawing in during autumn (c.f. Hindu Divali), or new life in spring (c.f. Zoroastrian and Bahá'í New Years). So whatever their pedigree, festival times would seem useful points of contact between traditions, especially when connected to the changing seasons we all share.

Themes that struck me during the Conversation included the value of direct experience, whether this is individual 'religious experience' as traditionally understood ('mystical' or 'numinous'), shared experience, a sense of genuine participation in nature, or the power of ritual in creating experience. For women in particular, seeing experience as a source of authority is important, as few women have had positions of authority within religious traditions until relatively recently.

The third section of the book illustrates the potential of shared ritual in bringing different traditions together in a way that theological debate may not. Another important theme, dealt with in many of the chapters of this book, is the value of myth and story as the language through which spiritual ideas and experiences are expressed.

What next?

Participants felt that we had only just begun our Conversation, and that several areas could be explored further to positive effect.

These were identified as:

- Theology;
- Environmental activism;
- Creativity and the arts;
- Young people.

Subgroups hope to work on these topics. Whether the enthusiasm of an intense weekend will last once back in our own contexts and busy lives remains to be seen – but as the first step was taken, there should be a second.

Has the Pagan/Christian dialogue anything to offer those who do not identify with either tradition, or are 'non-religious'? I would suggest that realising that environmental activism benefits from a deep ('spiritual'?) motivation, that ritual and ceremony can have transforming power, that story and myth contain important truths, and that people who do not agree about some fundamental aspects of reality can nevertheless enjoy each others' company, share ritual, and work together, can be useful for everyone. If we edit out, or reinterpret, or replace (with 'earth' or 'people' or 'all beings'), the 'spirit(s)', most people, 'religious' or 'non-religious' could join in the Druid promise (see chapter 10):

> We swear by peace and love to stand,
> heart to heart and hand in hand.
> Mark, O Spirit(s), and hear us now,
> confirming this, our sacred vow.
> So may it be!

Notes

Notes for Chapter 8

1   From *The Charge of the Goddess,* by Doreen Valiente. *The Charge of the Goddess* is traditionally copied by hand by Wiccan initiates, from the handwritten *Book of Shadows* of their initiator which is, of course, a secret text. For academic purposes published versions are available in various sources, but I suggest: Valiente, D., (2014). It can also be found in Griffyn (2002, p.41).

2   My use of the words Pagan and Paganism can be taken, for the purposes of this chapter, to mean 'contemporary British Paganism' as opposed to the many other types.

3   For scholarly contextualisation of ritual as 'performative' see the following: Grimes, R.L., (2012) Grimes, R.L., (2006) Schechner, R., (2002) Schieffelin, E., (1998).

4   Ceridwen and her cauldron are mentioned in the *Tale of Taliesin* found in *The Black Book of Carnarvon* – the manuscript is currently part of the collection of the National Library of Wales, where it is catalogued as NLW Penarth MS 1. For a translation into English see: Guest, Lady C., (1906). An accessible extract can be found in Barber (1999, pp.146-152).

5   The poem *Mythopoea*, Tolkien (1964), begins *'To one [C.S. Lewis] who said that myths were lies and therefore worthless, even though 'breathed through silver'*. For attribution of the quote to Lewis: Carpenter, H. (1978, p.43).

6   *The Pagan Federation* is an umbrella organisation (insofar as Pagans can be organised), which represents Pagans from diverse traditions. See http://www.paganfed.org

Notes for Chapter 9

7   Both Earth Spirituality paths such as Druidry and Paganism, but also naturalists, ecologists, permaculture experts and

other assorted specialists.

8 I see five great separations from nature beginning with our shift as a species from food gatherers to food producers, the Reformation and Enlightenment, the Industrial Revolution and the agricultural revolution of the 1970s, but in my experience of facilitating nature connection exercises (mostly games) it takes 15 minutes and very little instruction to undo the separation.

9 *Lectio Divina*, literally Divine Reading, is a simple exercise typically using a passage of scripture. The first reading, an overview of the whole piece, is followed by a second where the reader allows a word or line to capture their attention, which may develop into contemplative prayer or dialogue with God.

10 The exercise can be found at: www.mysticchrist.co.uk /sensio_divina

11 Photos of the remains and the gathering can be found at: www.mysticchrist.co.uk/sunken_hundreds

12 As indeed it does need controlling if you're going to continue to do the basics such as feed eight billion people with the current agricultural model (permaculture is one alternative that doesn't attempt to 'control' nature). This is the big move, from participation to control, resulted from the first separation from nature when humans shifted from food gatherers to food producers roughly 10,000 years ago. The shift, however, missed areas of the planet (such as Australia) safe from the climate change at the time where food gathering continued.

13 For example the garden or park, open grassland with the occasional tree or shrub – how different from the forest the land of the UK would become if left to its own devices. I like the notion that we're mimicking here the savannah or prairie of our ancient past, where the first *Homo sapiens* lived, as some sort of environmental comfort blanket.

14   The soul or spirit of a place (or for some Pagans, local deity).

15   For reasons too complex to go into here I question whether the annual agricultural system has the same advantages for nature connection as it is based on a nature-control paradigm. This, I suggest, also has a huge impact on any cosmology or belief system developing under its influence. An argument I make in more detail in the first chapter of Stanley, 2013.

16   www.permaculture.org.uk

17   The 'Palio' lifestyle, which is developing momentum, has most prominence as a diet, but is much more far reaching, influencing everything from non-food products in the house to 'bare foot' exercise to child rearing. And of course a search for 'Palio Spirituality' delivers many results. For an intro-duction see: http://nyti.ms/XxngIj

18   www.childrenandnature.org

Note for Chapter 10

19   This can be viewed on YouTube at TheOldGreyWolfTest, 2012. *Paralympics 2012 Druid Ritual.* [online] Available at: <https://www.youtube.com/watch?v=eNE8PTgsjWk> [Accessed 08 October 2014].

Notes for Chapter 11

20   Carmina Gadelica, or *Ortha Nan Gaidheal*, meanings Songs of The Gael, a collection of hymns and incantations from the Western Isles of Scotland, collected by Alexander Carmichael (Carmichael, 1900).

21   Each 'branch' of Forest Church is named after its location, usually in a simple way, such as East Midlands Forest Church. We wanted a name that said something deeper about the location, and our area just south of Birmingham and North of Stratford is the site of the old Royal Forest of Arden. We abandoned Forest of Arden Forest Church, with

its surfeit of 'forests' in favour of Ancient Arden Forest Church.

22 'Everything that is is *in* God and God is *in* all things and yet God is not identical with the universe.' (McFague, 1993, p.149)

23 It is our hope to publish these explorations and rituals soon. In the meantime we have recently released a song book and CD with the music written for these eight seasonal festivals (Eve-Cudby, 2014c).

24 Thich Nhat Hanh, 2013, p.24-5.

25 Throughout much of what I will say, I am aware that it is the shortcomings of Christian attitudes that I keep focussing on, and I hope Pagan readers do not feel excluded by this. Stuck between worlds, I feel somewhat unqualified to speak to or for either polarity, but I do appreciate the need that many Christians feel to 'get it right' theologically. Although I may no longer share this concern, I have sought to offer possibilities as well as questions for folk of a less heterodox nature, to engage with this ritual project or at least grasp the difficulties and begin to find their own way through. Many of the suggestions I will offer as facilitating shared ritual for the service of the earth are more or less already central to Pagan practice.

26 Rather than Christians viewing this as a challenge for *non*-Christians in inter-religious conversation as Harvey does, I'm suggesting that the *Solus Christus,* is rather more a stumbling block for *Christians* in dialogue (Harvey, 1997, p.223).

27 A mage is a practitioner of magic.

28 Interestingly, contemporary Pagans sometimes replicate, or re-configure this distinction between religion and magic (Greer, 2007, p.232). In addition, the word 'magick' is often used by practitioners to distance their activities from illusory magic. There is not the space here, however, to

explore these dialectics too deeply, and magic is used in a very broad sense in this work.

29 She arrives at this through the critique of the western reductionist split between spirit and matter, where the 'spiritual' is an explanatory category employed by ancient and indigenous peoples. This is combined with the critique of scientific materialist certainty offered by quantum theory. She particular draws on the work of Karen Barad, and Brian Latour.

Notes for Chapter 12

30 See http://www.sofn.org.uk/
31 See http://livingreligion.co.uk

References

References for Chapter 1

Armstrong, K. 2000. *The Battle for God*. London: HarperCollins. Relevant extract [on-line] Available at http://www.nytimes.com/books/first/a/armstrong-battle.html [Accessed 2 October 2014].

Cush, D., 1994. A suggested typology of positions on religious diversity. *Journal of Beliefs and Values,* 15 (2), pp.18-21.

Isherwood, L. and McEwan, D., 1993. *Introducing Feminist Theology*. Sheffield: Sheffield Academic Press.

Murray, M., 1921. *The Witch Cult in Western Europe*. [online] Available at http://www.sacred-texts.com/pag/murray.htm and http://www.sacred-texts.com/pag/wcwe/index.htm [Accessed 1 October 2014].

Race, A., 1983. *Christians and Religious Pluralism*. London: SCM.

Reid-Bowen, P., 2007. *Goddess as Nature: Towards a Philosophical Theology*. Aldershot: Ashgate.

Thepaganstudygroup, 2014. *Pop Culture Paganism: An Introduction*. [online] Available at: http://thepaganstudy-grouppage.tumblr.com/post/75580019817/pop-culture-paganism-an-introduction [Accessed 6 October 2014).

References for Chapter 2

Behringer, W., 2004, *Witches and Witch-Hunts*. Cambridge: Polity.

Bosch, D., 1993. *Transforming Mission*. New York: Orbis.

Brown, M., 2006. *How Christianity Came to Britain and Ireland*. London: Lion.

Brown, T., 1997. Clearances and Clearings: Deforestation in Mesolithic/Neolithic Britain, *Oxford Journal of Archaeology* 16 (2), pp.133–146.

Budin, S., 2008. *The Myth of Sacred Prostitution in Antiquity*. New York: Cambridge University Press.

Chadwick, H,. 1967. *The Early Church*. London: Penguin.

Day, J., 2004. Does the Old Testament refer to sacred prostitution and did it actually exist in Ancient Israel? In C. McCarthy & J.F. Healey, eds, *Biblical and Near Eastern Essays: Studies in Honour of Kevin J. Cathcart*. London: Continuum International Publishing Group. pp.2-21.

De Paor, L., 1993. *Saint Patrick's World: The Christian Culture of Ireland's Apostolic Age*. Dublin: Four Courts, pp.154-97.

Donovan, V., 2001. *Christianity Re-Discovered*. London: SCM.

Douglas, M., 1973. *Natural Symbols*. Harmondsworth: Penguin.

Driver, T.F., 2005. The Case for Pluralism. In Hick J., Knitter, P. *The Myth of Christian Uniqueness*. Eugene, OR: Wipf & Stock pp 203-218.

Eliade M., 1976. *Occultism, Witchcraft, and Cultural Fashions: Essays in Comparative Religion*. Chicago: Chicago University Press.

Harvey, G., 1997. *Listening People, Speaking Earth*. London: Hurst & Co.

Hick J., Knitter, P. 200.5 *The Myth of Christian Uniqueness*. Eugene, or: Wipf & Stock.

Hollinghurst, S., 2010. *Mission-Shaped Evangelism*. Norwich: Canterbury Press.

Hutton, R., 1991. *The Pagan Religions of the Ancient British Isles: Their Nature and Legacy*. Oxford, UK and Cambridge, US: Blackwell.

Hutton, R., 2007. *The Druids*. London: Hambledon Continuum.

Kamen, H., 1997. *The Spanish Inquisition: A Historical Revision*. Newhaven: Yale University Press.

Lee A.D., 2013. *From Rome to Byzantium AD 363 to 565: The Transformation of Ancient Rome*. Oxford: Oxford University Press.

McCurley, F., 1983 *Ancient Myths and Biblical Faith*. Philadelphia: Fortress Press.

Moberly, R., W. 2001 edition *The Old Testament of the Old*

Testament: Patriarchal Narratives and Mosaic Yahwism. Eugene, OR: Wipf and Stock.

Niebuhr, H. R., 1951 *Christ and Culture.* New York: Harper.

Pannikar, R., 2005. The Jordan, the Tiber and the Ganges in Hick, J., Knitter, P. *The Myth of Christian Uniqueness.* Eugene, OR: Wipf & Stock pp.89-116.

Rawlings, H., 2006 *The Spanish Inquisition.* London: Blackwell Publishing.

Scarre, G. Callow J., 2001 *Witchcraft and Magic in Sixteenth and Seventeenth-Century Europe* (second ed.). Basingstoke: Palgrave.

Stanley, B. 2013 *Forest Church.* Llangurig: Mystic Christ Press.

Stanley, B. & Hollinghurst, S. (eds.), 2014 *Earthed.* Llangurig: Mystic Christ Press.

Wessels, A., 1994 *Europe: Was it Ever Really Christian?* London SCM Press.

Wyatt, N., 2003 *Religious Texts from Ugarit.* Sheffield: Sheffield Academic Press.

References for Chapter 3

Grimes, R., 2013. Performance is currency in the deep world's gift economy: an incantatory riff for a global medicine show. In G. Harvey, ed. *Handbook of Contemporary Animism.* Durham: Acumen, pp.501-12.

Harvey, G., 2007. *Listening People, Speaking Earth: Contemporary Paganism.* (2nd edition). London: Hurst.

Harvey, G., 2013. *Food, Sex and Strangers: Understanding religion as everyday life.* Durham: Acumen.

Latour, B., 1993. *We Have Never Been Modern,* Cambridge: Harvard University Press.

Rorty, R. M., 1998. *Pragmatism as Romantic Polytheism. In:* M. Dickstein, ed. *The Revival of Pragmatism: New Essays on Social Thought, Law, and Culture.* Durham, NC: Duke University Press, pp.21-36.

Snyder, G., 1990. *The Practice of the Wild*. New York: North Point Press.

Wade, N., 2008. Bacteria Thrive in Inner Elbow; No Harm Done. *New York Times* (23 May), [on-line] Available at www. nytimes.com/2008/05/23/science/23gene.html [accessed 31 March 2014].

References for Chapter 4

Ainsworth, W.H., 1843. *Windsor Castle*. London: Henry Colburn.

Grahame, K., 1908. *The Wind in the Willows*. London: Methuen.

Graves, R., 1948. *The White Goddess*. London: Faber&Faber.

Hutton, R., 1999. *The Triumph of the Moon: A History of Modern Pagan Witchcraft*. Oxford: Oxford University Press.

Leland, C.G., 1899. *Aradia*. London: David Nutt.

Machen, A., 1894. *The Great God Pan*. London: John Lane.

References for Chapter 5

Brueggemann, W., 1986. *Hopeful Imagination: Prophetic Voices in Exile*. Minneapolis: Fortress.

Carr-Gomm, P., 2006.*The Druid Way*. Loughborough: Thoth Publications.

Daniel, N., 1975.*The Arabs and Mediaeval Europe*. London/Beirut: Longman.

Hoyt, R., 2009. *Journey to the Sea*. [online] Available at: http://journeytothesea.com/mythos-logos/ [Accessed 29th August 2014].

Hutton, R.B., 2009. *The Pagan Religions of the Ancient British Isles*. Oxford: Blackwell.

Hutton, R.B., 2013. *Pagan Britain*. London: Yale.

MacLeod, G.F., 1985. *The Whole Earth Shall Cry Glory*. Iona: Wild Goose Publications.

McGowan, L., 2010. *Faerie Lore*. [online] Available at: http://www.technogypsie.com/faerie/?p=7 [Accessed 29th August 2014].

Michell, J., 1997. *New Light on the Ancient Mystery of Glastonbury*.

Glastonbury: Gothic Image Publications.

Michell, J., 2008. *The Traveller's Guide to Sacred England*. Glastonbury: Gothic Image Publications.

Yeats, W.B., 2011. *The Land of Heart's Desire*. Marston Gate: Aeterna.

References for Chapter 6

Carr-Gomm, P. 2002. *In the Grove of the Druids: The Druid Teachings of Ross Nichols*. London: Watkins.

Carr-Gomm P., 2006. *What Do Druids Believe?* London: Granta.

'Davem' (Amazon Reviewer), 2013 *Customer Review of Forest Church by Bruce Stanley*. [online] Available at: http://www.amazon.co.uk/product-reviews/B00BF09HEO/ref=cm_cr_dp_see_all_btm?ie=UTF8&showViewpoints=1&sortBy=bySubmissionDateDescending [Accessed 5 March 2014].

Davidson, F. 1998. *The Language of Birds*. [CD] Ardgour: Watercolour Music (WCMCD017).

Erskine, B., 2005. Personal communication to author, *cited in* P. Carr-Gomm, 2006. *What Do Druids Believe?* London: Granta, p.7.

Pearson, Joanne. 2007. *Wicca and the Christian Heritage: Ritual, Sex and Magic* London: Routledge.

Pinkola Estes, C., 2008. *Women Who Run with the Wolves*. London: Rider.

Stanley, B., 2013. *Forest Church: A Field Guide to Nature Connection for Groups and Individuals* Llangurig: Mystic Christ Press.

Wikipedia, 2014. *Syncretism*. [online] Available at: http://en.wikipedia.org/wiki/Syncretism [Accessed 2 November 2014].

References for Chapter 7

Chodron, P., 1997. *When Things Fall Apart. Heart Advice for Difficult Times*. Boston, MA: Shambala Publications.

Christ, C. P., 1980. *Diving Deep and Surfacing: Women Writers on Spiritual Quest*. Boston, MA: Beacon.

Fox, M., 1988. *The Coming of the Cosmic Christ*. San Francisco, CA: Harper San Francisco.

Gormley A., 2005. Interview in *Third Way* magazine. March 2005.

Jung C.G., 1945. *The Philosophical Tree*. CW 13: Alchemical Studies. [online] Available at: http://psikoloji.fisek.com.tr/jung/shadow .htm [Accessed 5 October 2014].

Keller, C., 1990. Women Against Wasting the World. In: I. Diamond and G. Orenstein, ed. *Reweaving the World: The Emergence of Ecofeminism*. San Francisco CA: Sierra Club Books.

Newell J.P., 2008. *Christ of the Celts: The Healing of Creation*. Glasgow: Wild Goose Publications.

Radford Ruether, R., 1992. *Gaia and God*. San Francisco CA: Harper San Francisco.

Reid, L., 2005. *She Changes Everything: Seeking the Divine on a Feminist Path*. London: T&T Clark International.

Shihab Nye, N., 2008. *Tender Spot. Selected Poems*. Hexham: Bloodaxe Books.

Smith, C., 1987. *The Way of Paradox, Spiritual Life as taught by Meister Eckhart*. London: Darton Longman and Todd.

Teilhard de Chardin, P., 1978. *The Heart of Matter*, trans. Hague, R., London: Collins.

Thich Nhat Hanh, 1995. *Living Buddha, Living Christ*. New York, NY: Riverhead Books.

Ward, T., 2007. *The Celtic Wheel of the Year*. Alresford: O Books.

White K., 2003. *Open World. The Collected Poems 1960-2000*. Edinburgh: Birlinn.

Wickliffe E., 2009. *Historical View of W.C. Williams': 'No Ideas but in Things'* [online] Available at: http://triggerfishcritical review.com/historical-view-of-wcwilliams-no-ideas-but-in-things-by-ed-wickliffe/ [Accessed 5 October 2014].

Williams R., 2003 *Silence and Honey Cakes: The Wisdom of the Desert*. London: Lion Hudson.

References for Chapter 8

Barber, R., 1999. *Myths and Legends of the British Isles.* Woodbridge: Boydell.

Campbell, J., 2008. *Hero With a Thousand Faces.* 2nd ed., Novato, Canada. New World Library (first published 1949).

Carpenter, H. 1978. *The Inklings.* London. Allen & Unwin.

Graves, R. 1948., *The White Goddess.* London: Faber&Faber.

Griffyn, S., 2002. *Wiccan Wisdom Keepers.* Alreford: Godsfield Press.

Grimes, R.L., 2006. *Fiddling with Fiddler* in *Rite Out of Place.* Oxford: Oxford University Press.

Grimes, R.L., 2012. *Religion, Ritual, and Performance* in *Religion, Theatre, and Performance.* New York: Routledge.

Guest, Lady Charlotte. 1906. *The Mabinogion.* London: JM Dent & Sons.

Hutton, R. 1996. Stations of the Sun: A History of the Ritual Year in Britain. Oxford & New York: Oxford University Press.

Schechner, R., 2002. *Performance Studies. An Introduction.* New York: Routledge.

Schieffelin, E., 1998. Problematising Performance. In: F. Hughes-Freeland, ed. *Ritual, Performance, Media.* London: Routledge.

Tolkien, J.R.R., 1964. *Tree and Leaf.* London: Allen & Unwin.

Valiente, D., 2014. *The Charge of the Goddess, The Poetry of Doreen Valiente .* Milton Keynes: Centre for Pagan Studies.

References for Chapter 9

Cohen, M.J. 2007. *Reconnecting with Nature.* Apple Valley, MN: Finney/Ecopress.

Druidry.org. 2014. Training in Druidry. [on-line] Available at: http://www.druidry.org/druid-way/resources/training-druidry [Accessed 21st October, 2014).

Kaplan, S. 1995. The Restorative Benefits of Nature: Towards an Integrative Framework. *Journal of Environmental Psychology,* 15.

Kaplan, S., & Young, R.D., 2002. Towards a Better Understanding of Prosocial Behaviour: The Role of Evolution and Directed Attention. *Behavioural and Brain Sciences* 25(2).

Louv, R. 2010. *Last Child in the Woods.* London: Atlantic Books.

Louv, R. 2012. *The Nature Principle.* Chapel Hill, NC: Algonquin Books.

Stanley, B., 2013. *Forest Church: A Field Guide to Nature Connection for Groups and Individuals* Llangurig: Mystic Christ Press.

References for Chapter 10

Barber, R., 1999. *Myths and Legends of the British Isles.* Woodbridge: Boydell.

British Druid Order. 2014. [online] Available at: http://druidry.co.uk/ [Accessed October 21st 2014]

Carmichael, A. (1900). *Carmina Gadelica, Vol. 1* . Retrieved October 29th, 2014 from www.sacred-texts.com/neu/celt/cg1/cg107 5.htm

Hutton, R., 2003. *Witches, Druids and King Arthur.* London and New York: Hambledon.

Shallcrass, P. 2000. *Druidry: A Practical and Inspirational Guide.* London: Piatkus.

References for Chapter 11

Apffel-Marglin, F. (2011). *Subversive Spiritualities: How Rituals Enact The World.* New York: Oxford University Press.

Baker, J. (2004). Ritual as Strategic Practise. In P. Ward (Ed.), *The Rite Stuff: Ritual in Contemporary Christian Worship and Mission* (pp.85-95). Oxford: The Bible Reading Fellowship.

Bell, C. (1997). *Ritual Perspectives and Dimensions.* New York, Oxford: Oxford University Press.

Berry, T. (2009 Compiled). *The Sacred Universe.* New York: Columbia University Press.

Bowie, F. (2000). *The Anthropology of Religion.* Oxford: Blackwell Publishers Ltd.

Bradley, I. (2005). *Celtic Christianity: Making Myths and Chasing Dreams* (3rd ed.). Edinburgh: Edinburgh University Press.

Carmichael, A. (1900). *Carmina Gadelica, Vol. 1*. Retrieved October 29th, 2014 from www.sacred-texts.com/neu/celt/cg1/cg1075.htm

Corrigan, I. (2013). *Imbolc Rite - ADF Neopagan Druidism*. Retrieved January 29th, 2013 from http://www.adf.org/rituals/celtic/imbolc/imbolc.html

Cudby, P. (2014). *The Shaken Path: Understanding Paganism in the 21st Century*. Unpublished.

Davies, D. (2002). *Anthropology and Theology*. Oxford, New York: Berg.

D'Costa, G. (1998). Trinitarian différance and world religions: Postmodernity and the 'Other'. In U. King (Ed.), *Faith and Praxis in a Postmodern Age* (pp.28-46). London, New York: Cassell.

Eve and the Garden (Composer). (1996). *Quiet Earth And Shining Stars*. Free For Good.

Eve-Cudby, A. (2014b). *Into The Dark: Ancient Arden Forest Church Samhain 2014*. Tanworth in Arden: Ritualitas.

Eve-Cudby, A. (2014). The Sacred Circle: Elements of Ritual. In B. S. Hollinghurst (Ed.), *Earthed: Christian Perspectives on Nature Connection* (pp.244-271). Llangurig: Mystic Christ Press.

Eve-Cudby, A. (2014c). *The Song of the Wheel: Chants for The Forest Church Year From Ancient Arden Forest Church*. Tanworth in Arden: Ritualitas.

Greer, J. M. (2007). *The Druid Magic Handbook: Ritual Magic Rooted in the Living Earth*. San Francisco: Red Wheel/Weiser Press.

Greywolf. (2014). *Celebrating Planet Earth: A Conversation Between Christians Druids and Others*. Retrieved October 29, 2014 from http://greywolf.druidry.co.uk/2014/02/celebrating-planet-earth-a-conversation-between-christians-druids-and-others-1

Grimes, R. L. (2000). *Deeply into the Bone*. Berkeley and Los Angeles: University of California Press.

Grimes, R. L. (2010). *Ritual Criticism: Case Studies in Its Practice, Essays on Its Theory* (Second ed.). Waterloo: Ritual Studies International.

Grimes, R. L. (2014). *The Craft of Ritual Studies*. Oxford, New York: Oxford University Press.

Hanh, T. N. (2013). The Bells Of Mindfulness. In L. Vaughan-Lee (Ed.), *Spiritual Ecology: The Cry of the Earth* (pp.25-28). Point Reyes, CA: The Golden Sufi Centre.

Harvey, G. (2005). *Animism: Respecting the Living World*. London: C. Hurst & Co.

Harvey, G. (1997). *Listening People Speaking Earth: Contemporary Paganism*. London: C. Hurst & Co.

Hutton, R. (1996). *The Stations of the Sun: A History of the Ritual Year in Britain*. Oxford: Oxford University Press.

K. Amber, &. A. (2012). *Candlemas: Feast of Flames*. Woodbury, MN: Llewellyn Worldwide.

LaDuke, W. (2013). In The Time of the Sacred Places. In L. Vaughan-Lee (Ed.), *Spiritual Ecology: The Cry of the Earth* (pp.85-100). Point Reyes, CA: The Golden Sufi Centre.

Legg, V. (2014). Private Correspondence.

McFague, S. (1993). *The Body of God: An Ecological Theology*. Minneapolis: Fortress Press.

References for Chapter 12

Breuilly, E. and Palmer, M., 1992. *Christianity and Ecology*. London: WWF/Cassell.

Fox, M., 1992. *Creation Spirituality: Liberating Gifts for the Peoples of the Earth*. New York: HarperCollins.

Hutton, R. 1991. *The Pagan Religions of the Ancient British Isles*. Oxford: Blackwell.

McGrath, A., 2008. *The Open Secret: A New Vision for Natural Theology*. London: Hodder & Stoughton.

Pagan Federation, 2013. *Introduction to Paganism*. [online] Available at: http://www.paganfed.org/cms/index.php/paga

nism/introduction-to-paganism [Accessed 23 October 2014].

York, M. 2003. *Pagan Theology.* New York: New York University Press.

Tagore, R. (1961). *Towards Universal Man.* New York: Asia Publishing House.

White, L. (1967). The Historical Roots of our Ecological Crisis. *Science* 155, pp.1203-1207.

Moon Books invites you to begin or deepen your encounter with Paganism, in all its rich, creative, flourishing forms.

help healers and Reiki practitioners tap ancient healing wisdom.
Paperback: 978-1-84694-037-8 ebook: 978-1-84694-650-9

Pagan Portals – The Awen Alone
Walking the Path of the Solitary Druid
Joanna van der Hoeven
An introductory guide for the solitary Druid, *The Awen Alone* will
accompany you as you explore, and seek out your own place
within the natural world.
Paperback: 978-1-78279-547-6 ebook: 978-1-78279-546-9

A Kitchen Witch's World of Magical Herbs & Plants
Rachel Patterson
A journey into the magical world of herbs and plants, filled with
magical uses, folklore, history and practical magic. By popular
writer, blogger and kitchen witch, Tansy Firedragon.
Paperback: 978-1-78279-621-3 ebook: 978-1-78279-620-6

Shaman Pathways – The Druid Shaman
Exploring the Celtic Otherworld
Danu Forest
A practical guide to Celtic shamanism with exercises and
techniques as well as traditional lore for exploring the Celtic
Otherworld.
Paperback: 978-1-78099-615-8 ebook: 978-1-78099-616-5

Traditional Witchcraft for the Woods and Forests
A Witch's Guide to the Woodland with Guided Meditations and
Pathworking
Mélusine Draco
A Witch's guide to walking alone in the woods, with guided
meditations and pathworking.
Paperback: 978-1-84694-803-9 ebook: 978-1-84694-804-6

Wild Earth, Wild Soul
A Manual for an Ecstatic Culture
Bill Pfeiffer
Imagine a nature-based culture so alive and so connected,
spreading like wildfire. This book is the first flame...
Paperback: 978-1-78099-187-0 ebook: 978-1-78099-188-7

Naming the Goddess
Trevor Greenfield
Naming the Goddess is written by over eighty adherents and
scholars of Goddess and Goddess Spirituality.
Paperback: 978-1-78279-476-9 ebook: 978-1-78279-475-2

Shapeshifting into Higher Consciousness
Heal and Transform Yourself and Our World with Ancient
Shamanic and Modern Methods
Llyn Roberts
Ancient and modern methods that you can use every day to
transform yourself and make a positive difference in the world.
Paperback: 978-1-84694-843-5 ebook: 978-1-84694-844-2

Readers of ebooks can buy or view any of these bestsellers by
clicking on the live link in the title. Most titles are published in
paperback and as an ebook. Paperbacks are available in traditional
bookshops. Both print and ebook formats are available online.

Find more titles and sign up to our readers' newsletter at
http://www.johnhuntpublishing.com/paganism
Follow us on Facebook at https://www.facebook.com/MoonBooks
and Twitter at https://twitter.com/MoonBooksJHP